# THE NEW INTERNATIONAL WEBSTER'S UNITED STATES ATLAS

▲

## TRIDENT REFERENCE PUBLISHING

2006 EDITION

2006 Edition published by Trident Reference Publishing and distributed exclusively by
Trident Reference Publishing, 801 12th Avenue South, Suite 400, Naples Florida 34102 USA
www.tridentreference.com • email: sales@trident-international.com

Copyright © 2006 Trident Reference Publishing

All rights reserved

Copyright under the Universal Copyright Convention: the International Copyright Union;
Pan-American Conventions of Montevideo, Mexico, Rio de Janeiro, Buenos Aires and Havana

ISBN 1600811019
Printed in the United States of America

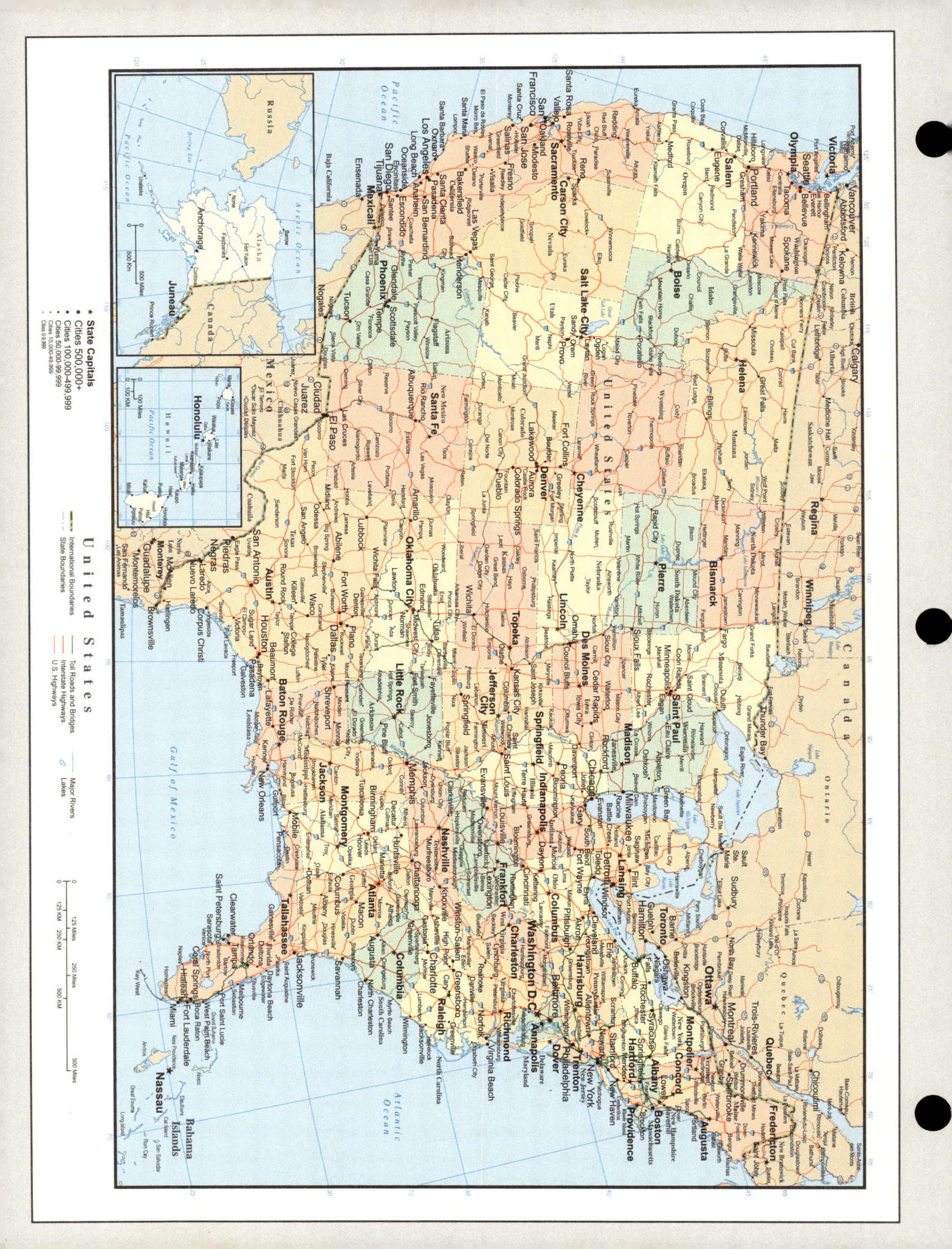

# United States

# ALABAMA

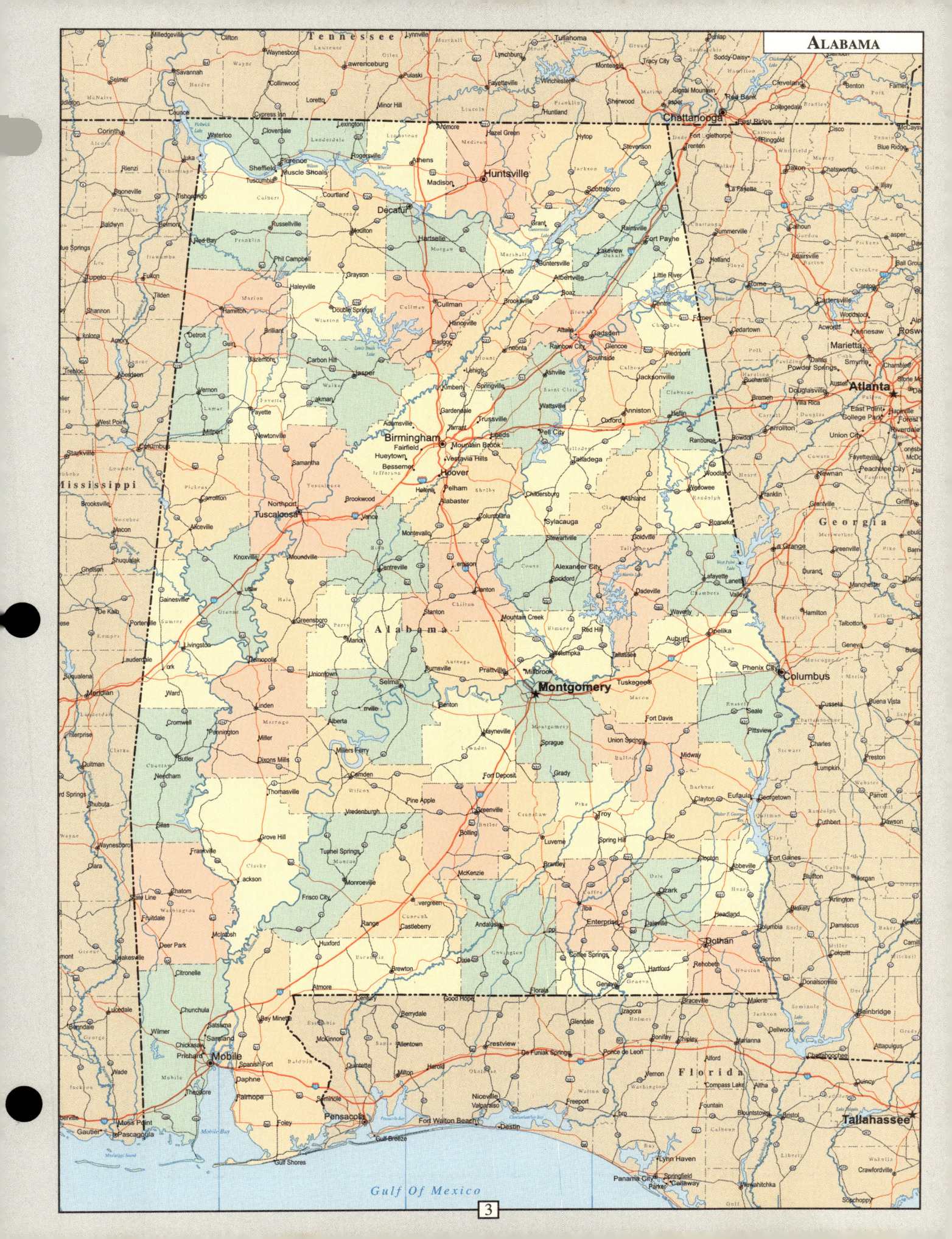

# ALASKA

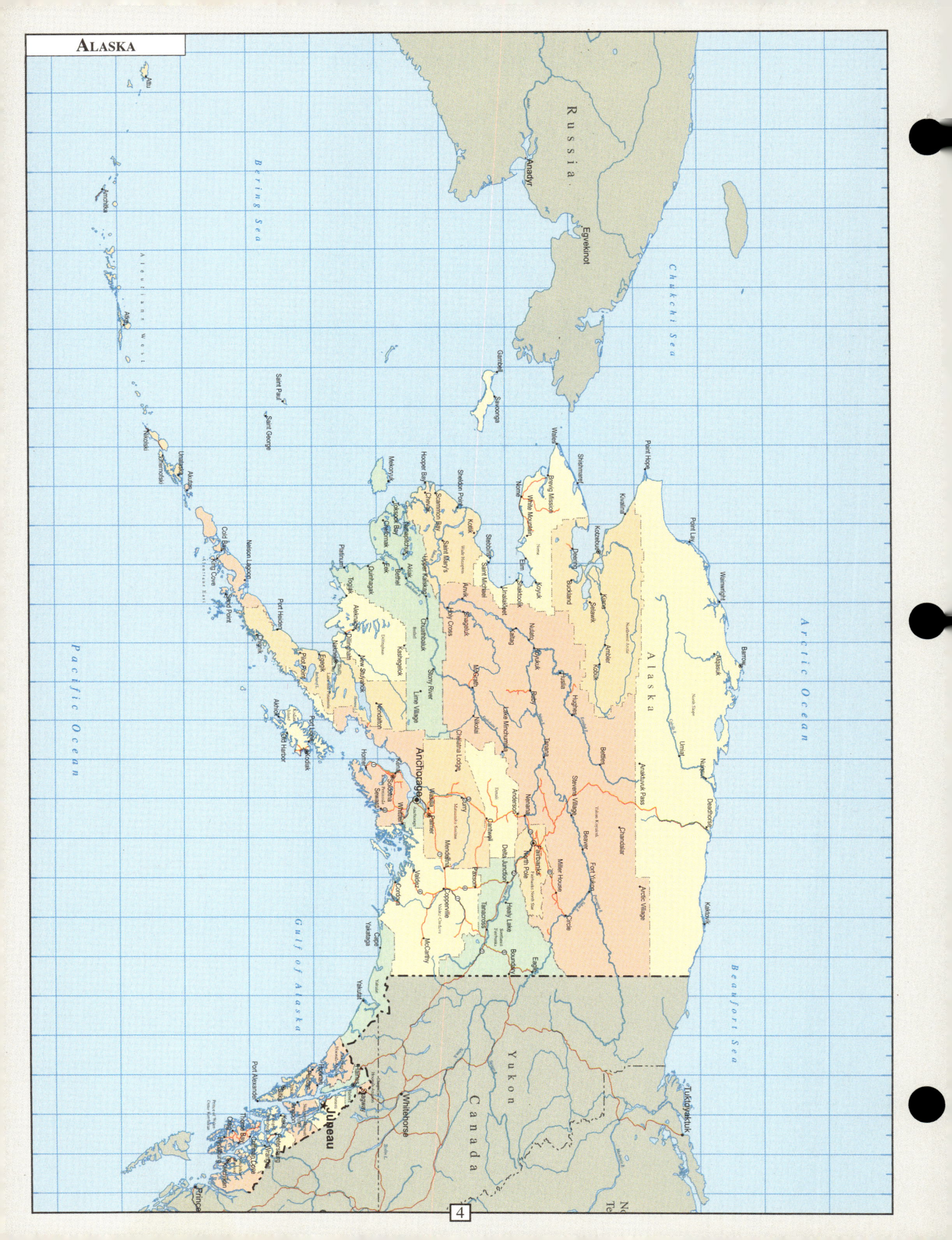

# ARIZONA

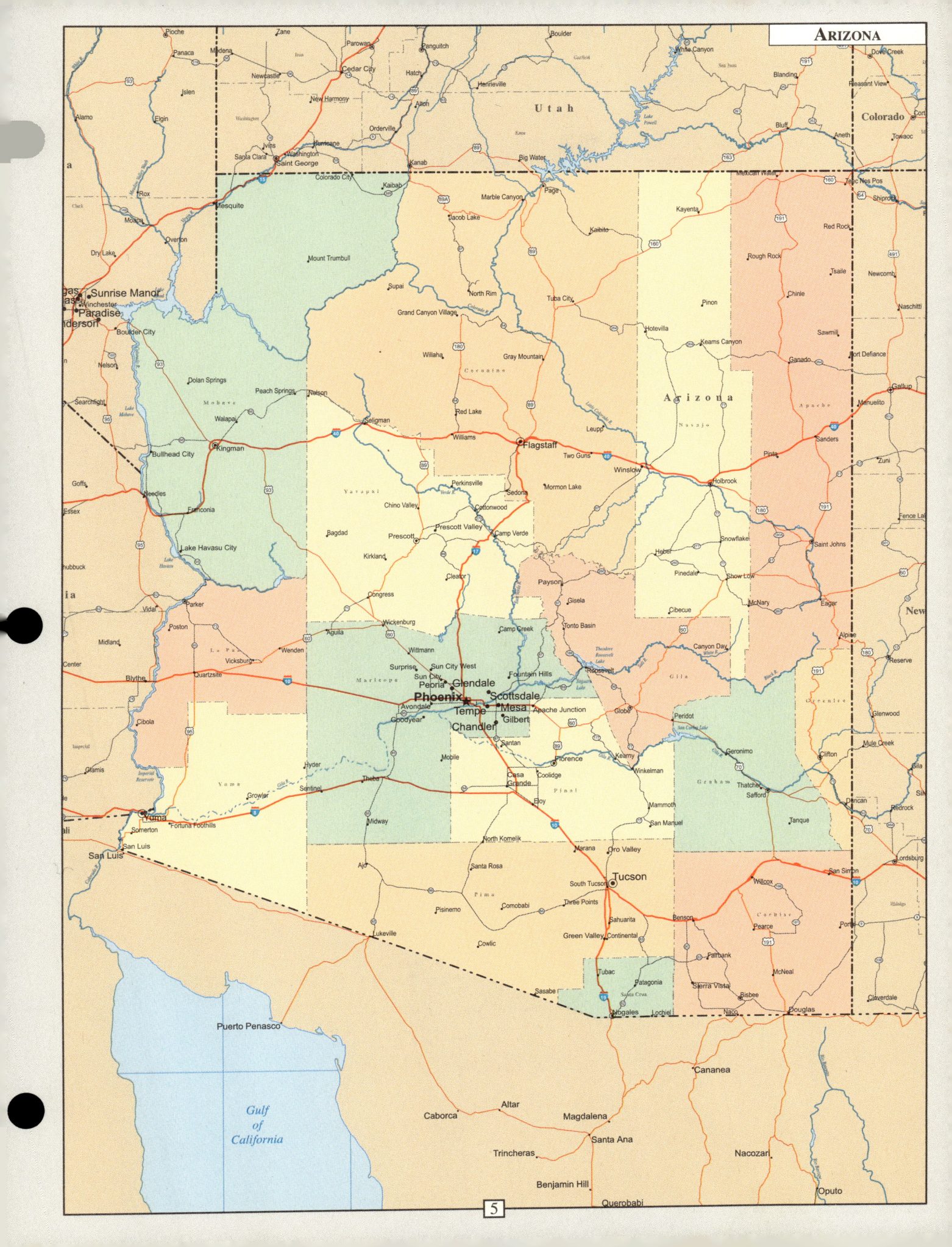

ARKANSAS

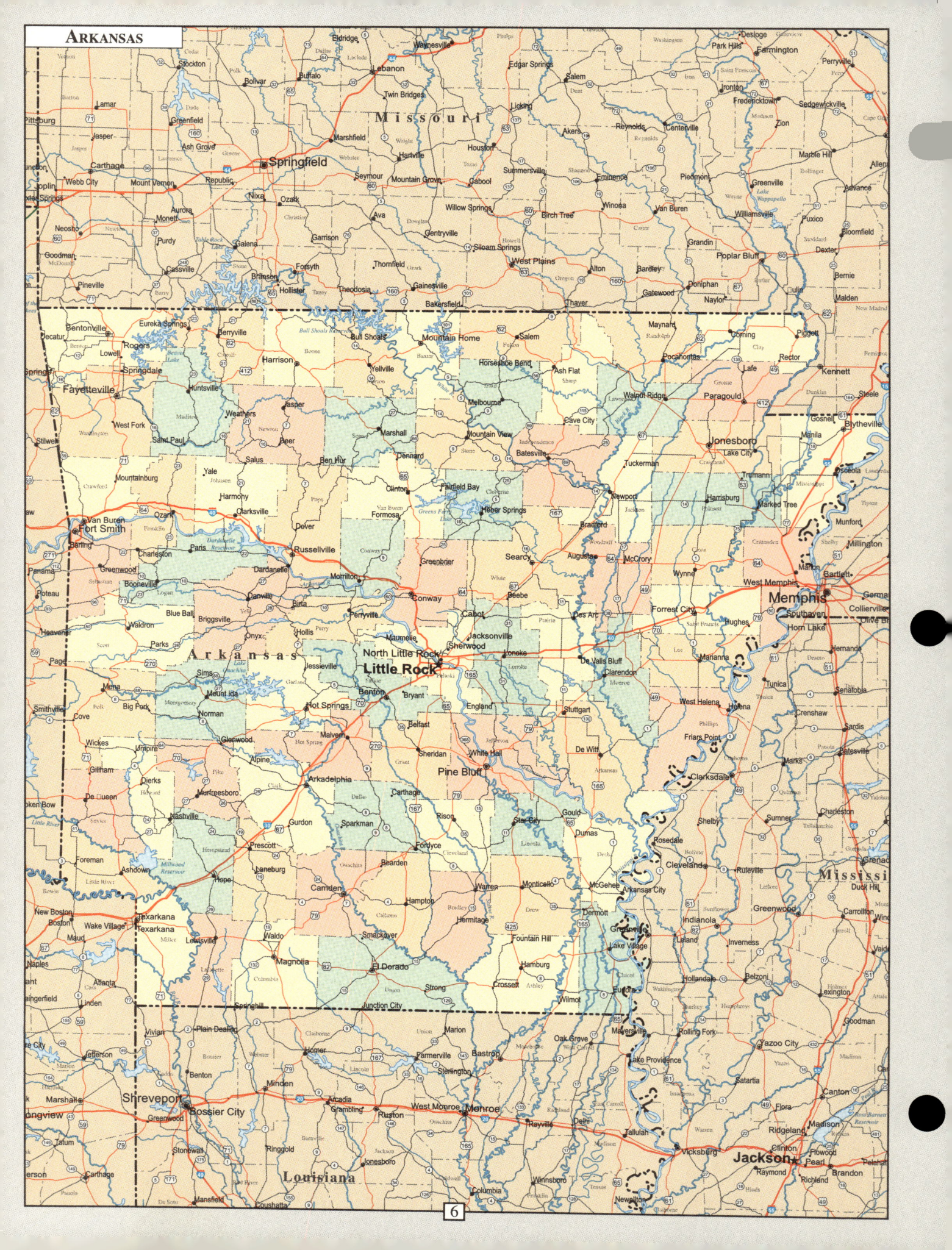

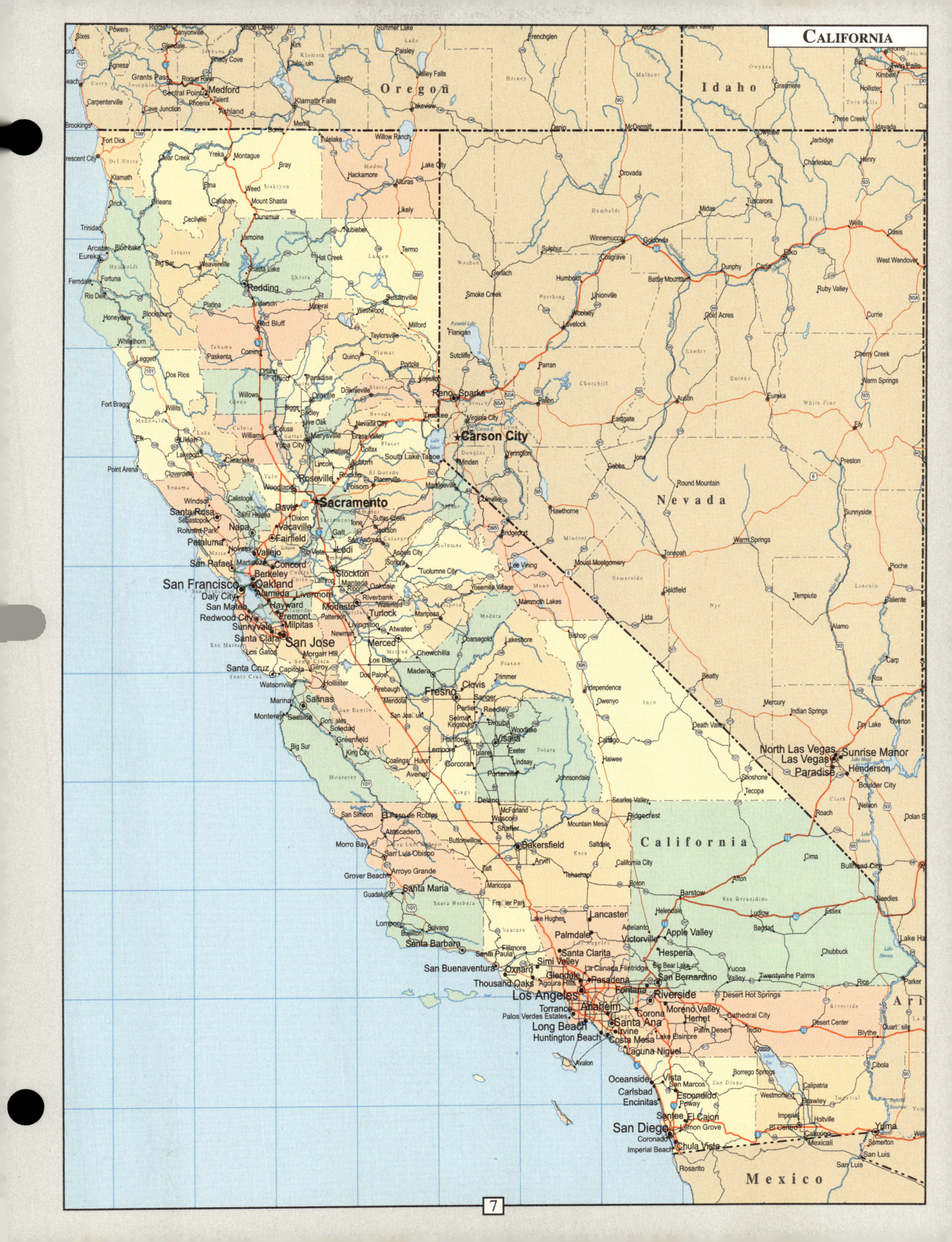

CALIFORNIA

# Colorado

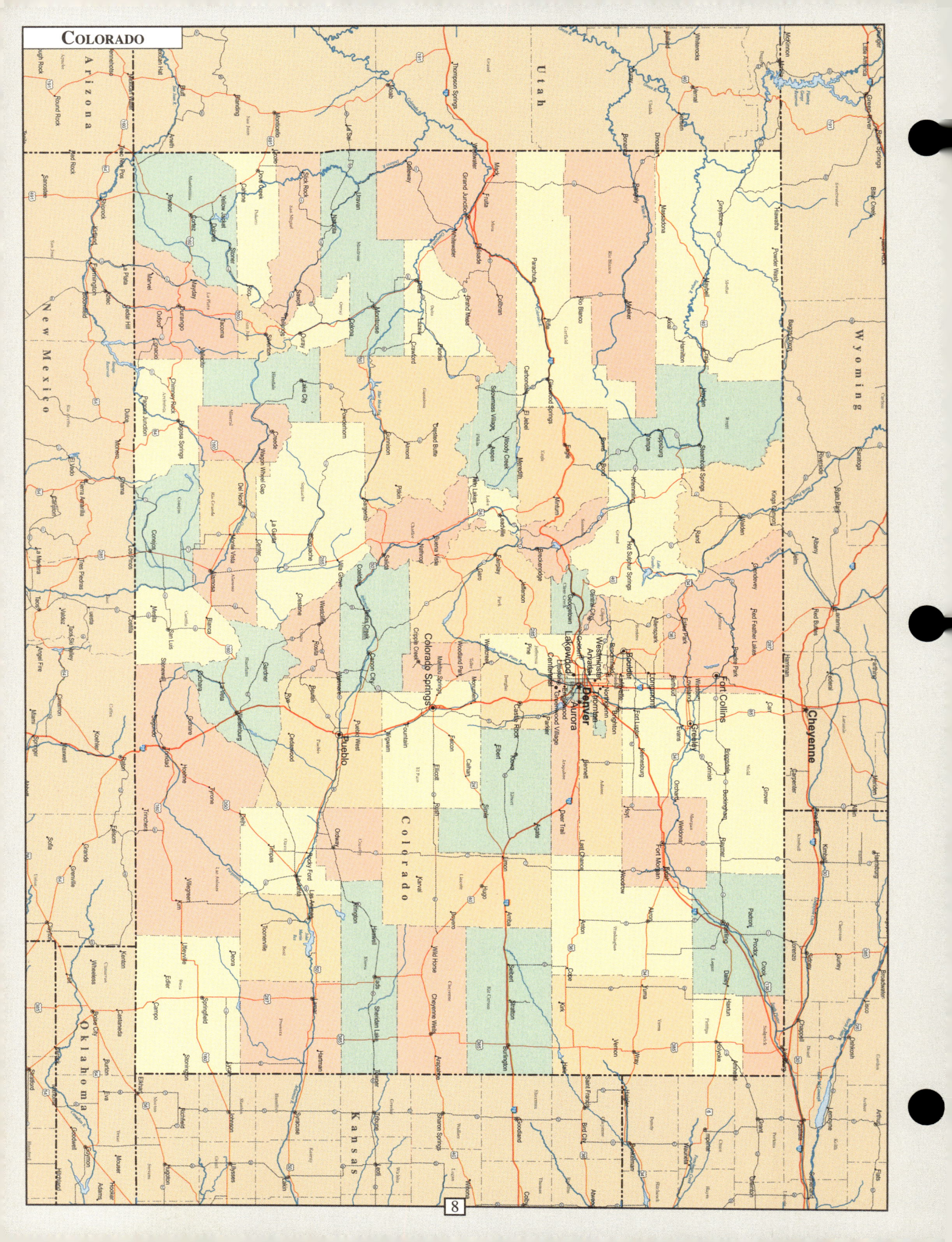

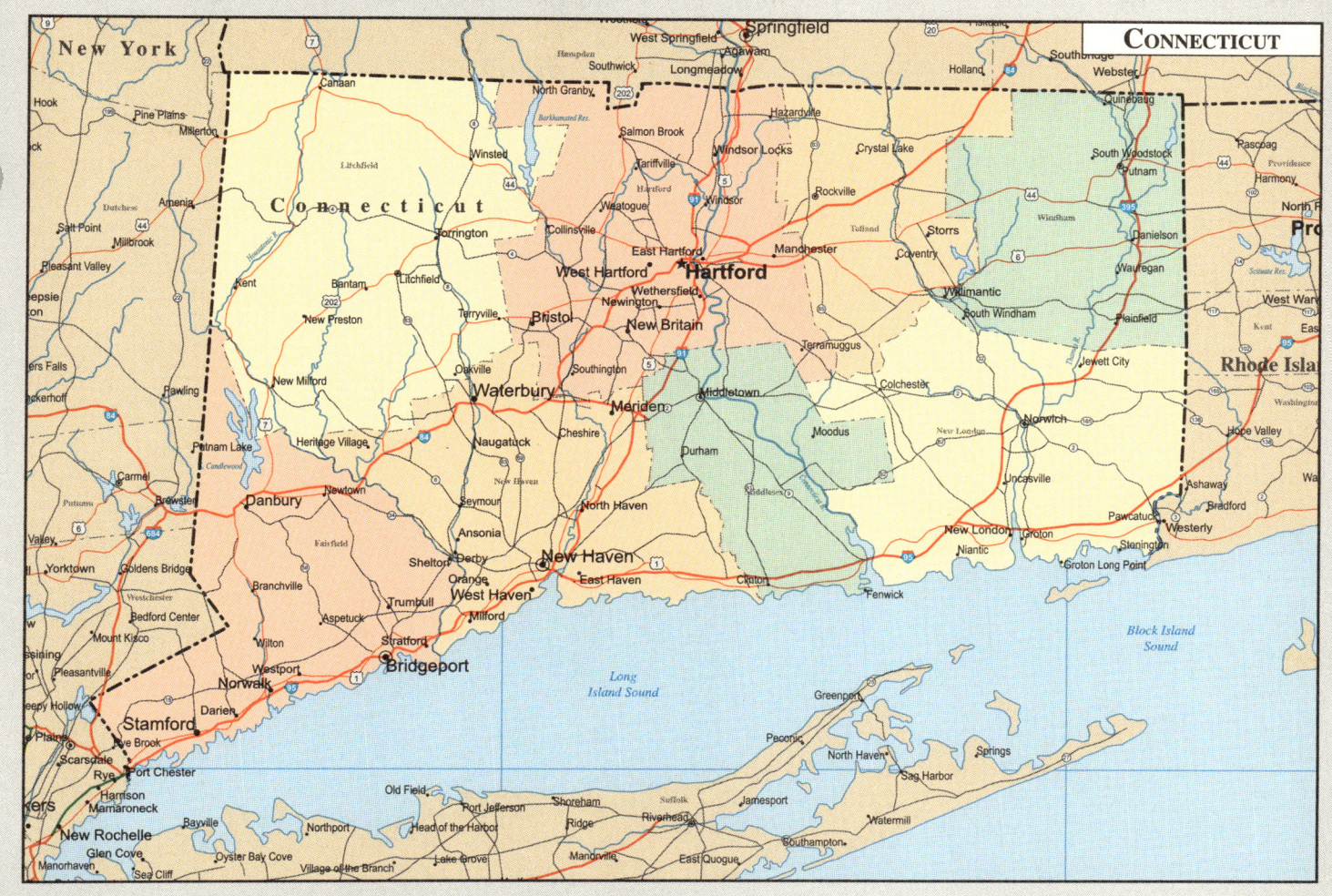

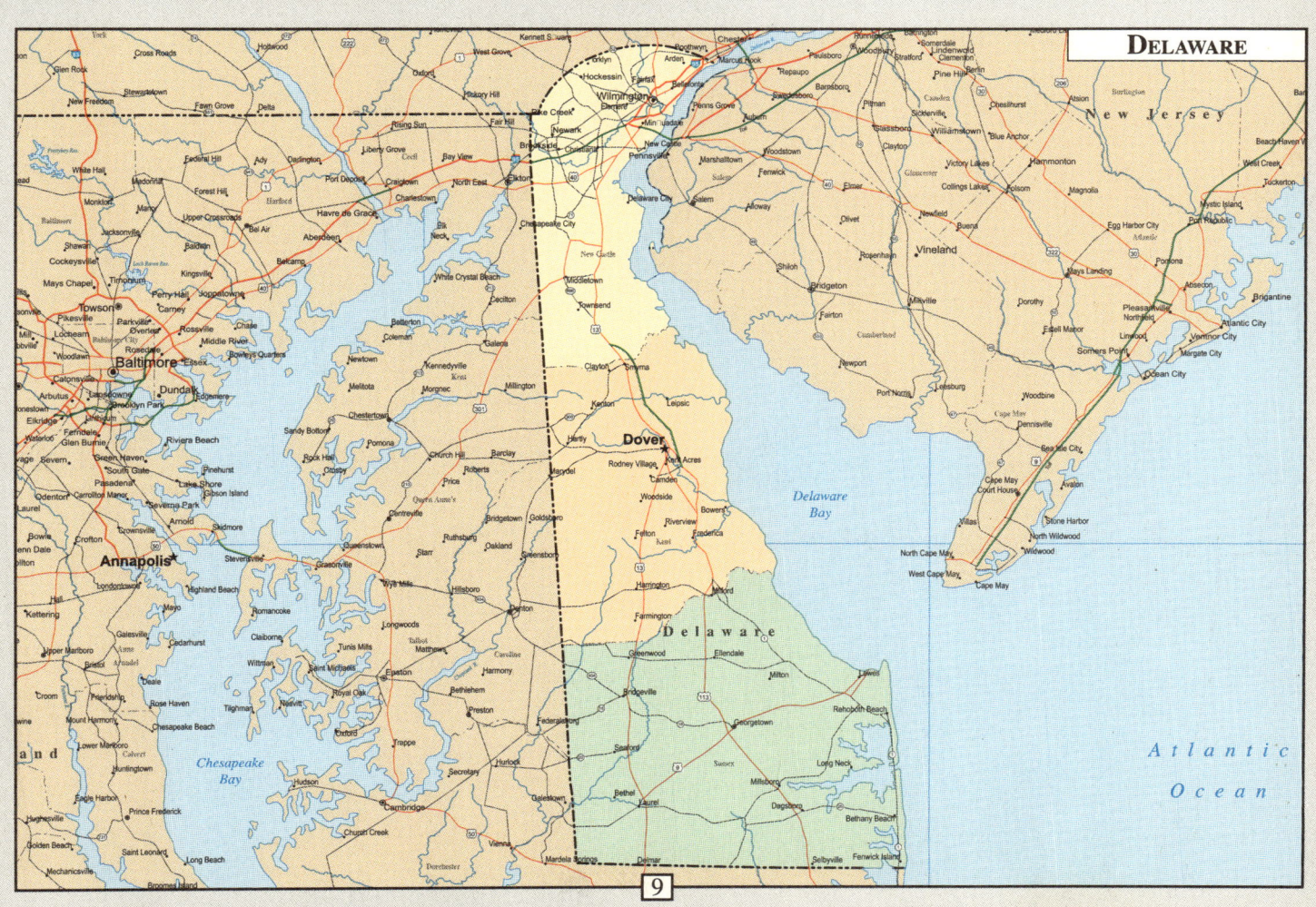

# CONNECTICUT

# DELAWARE

9

# Florida

# Georgia

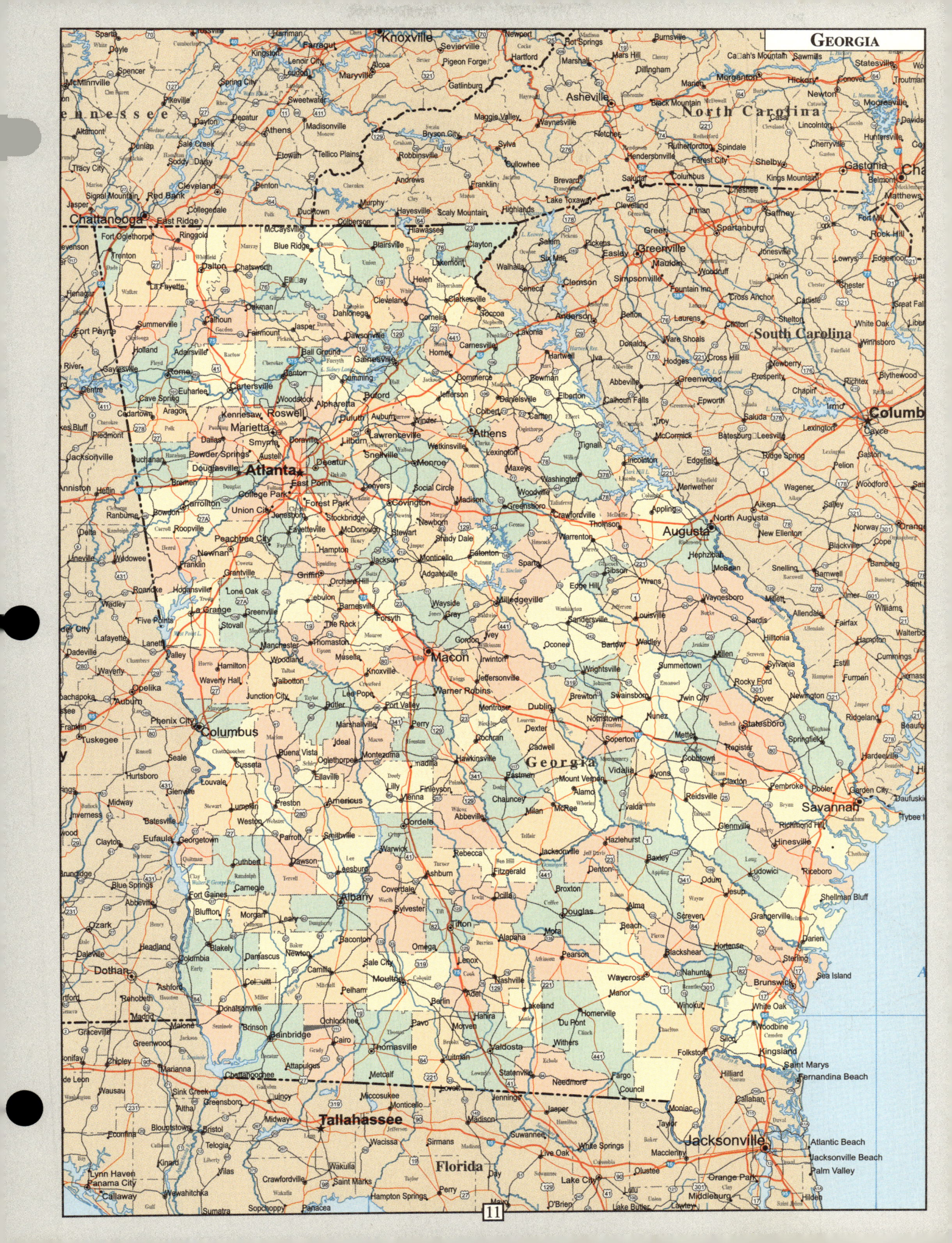

# Hawaii

# Idaho

# ILLINOIS

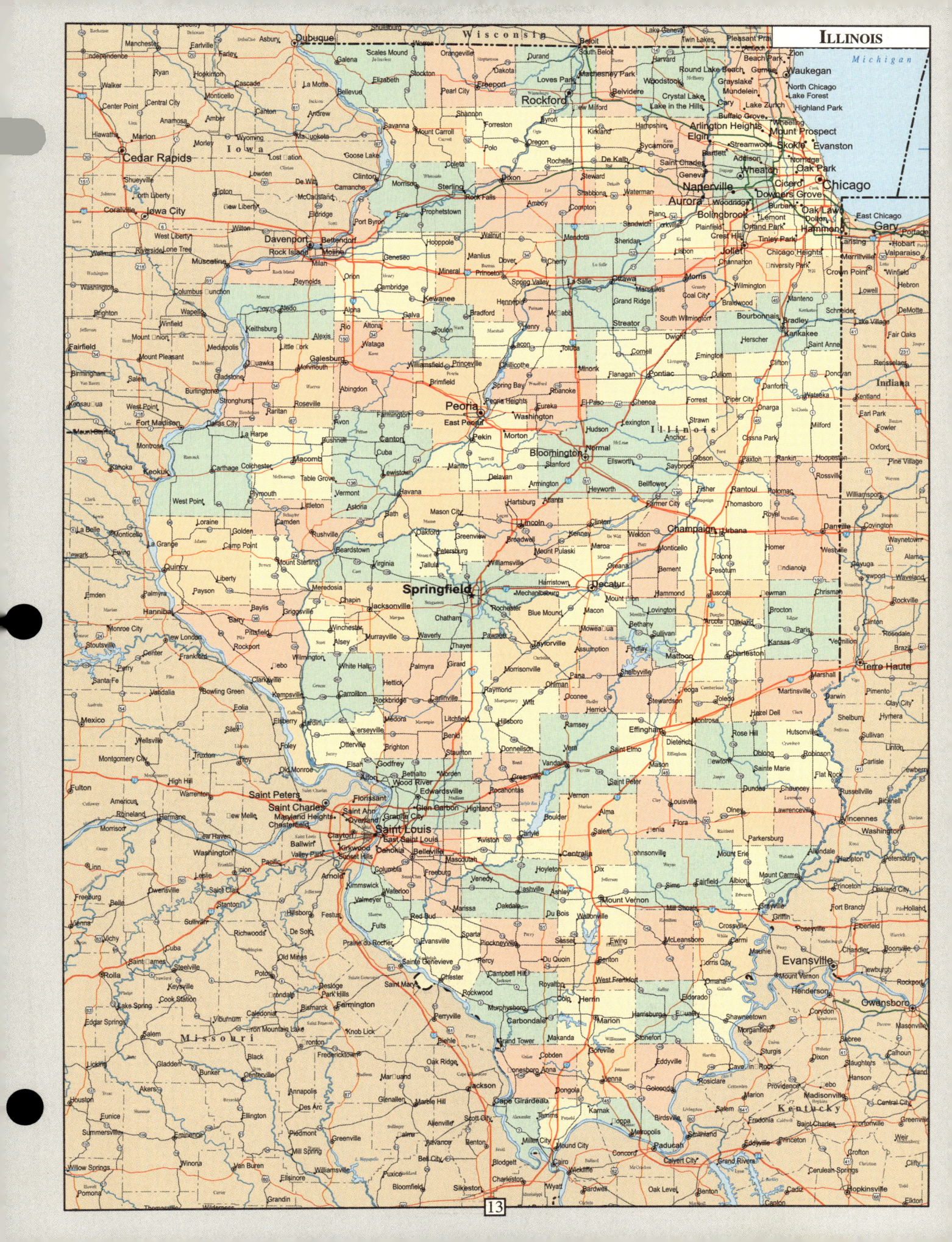

# INDIANA

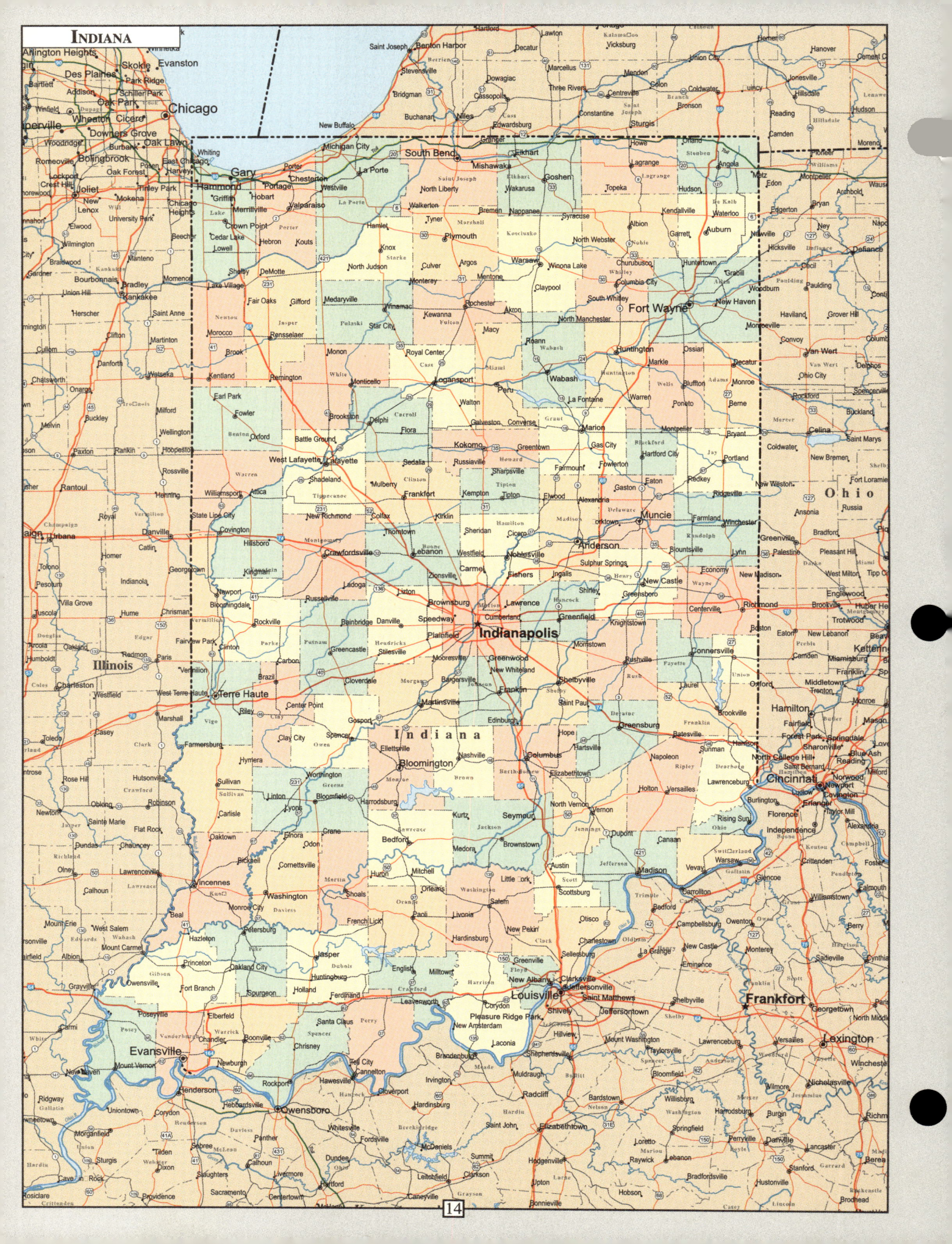

IOWA

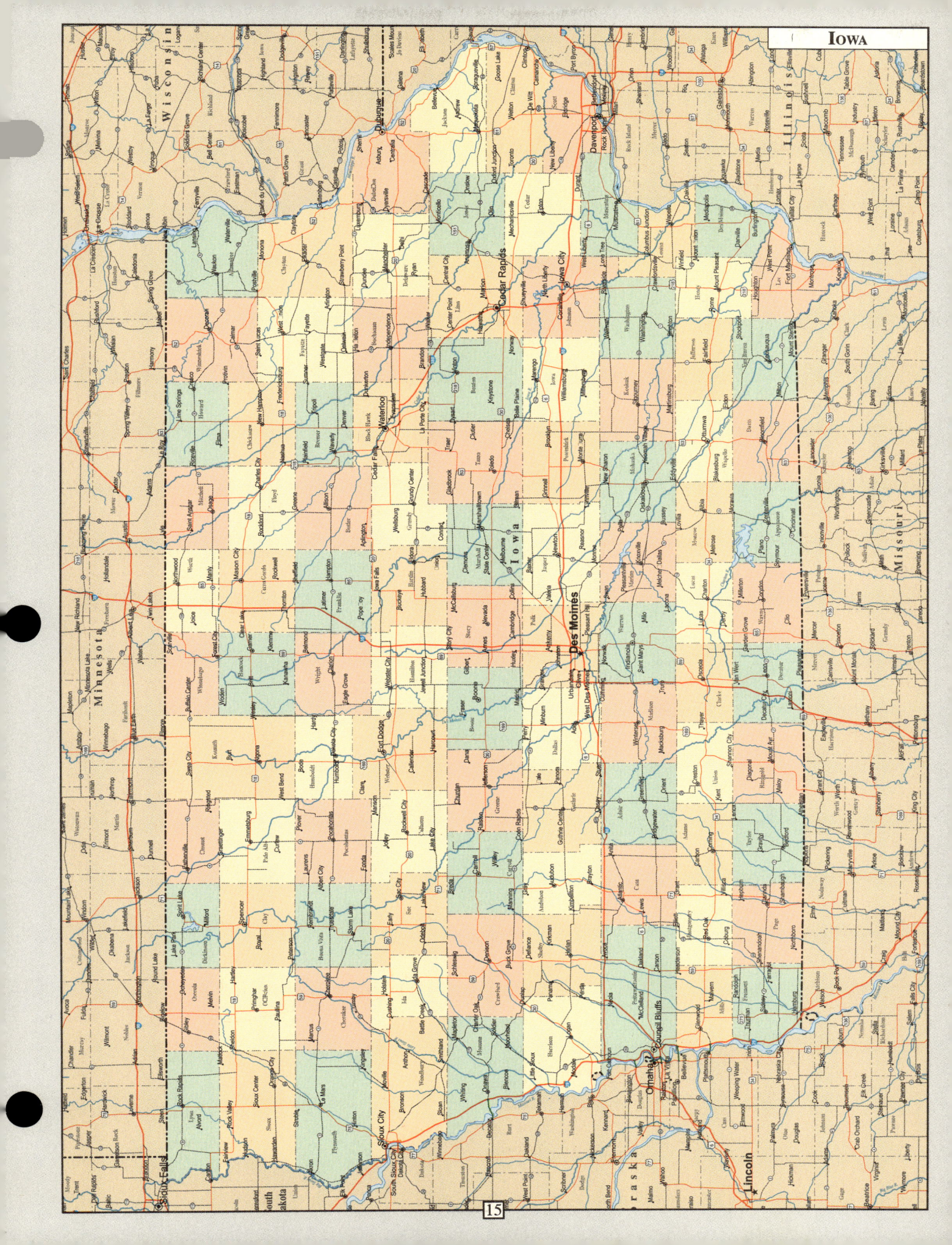

# Kansas

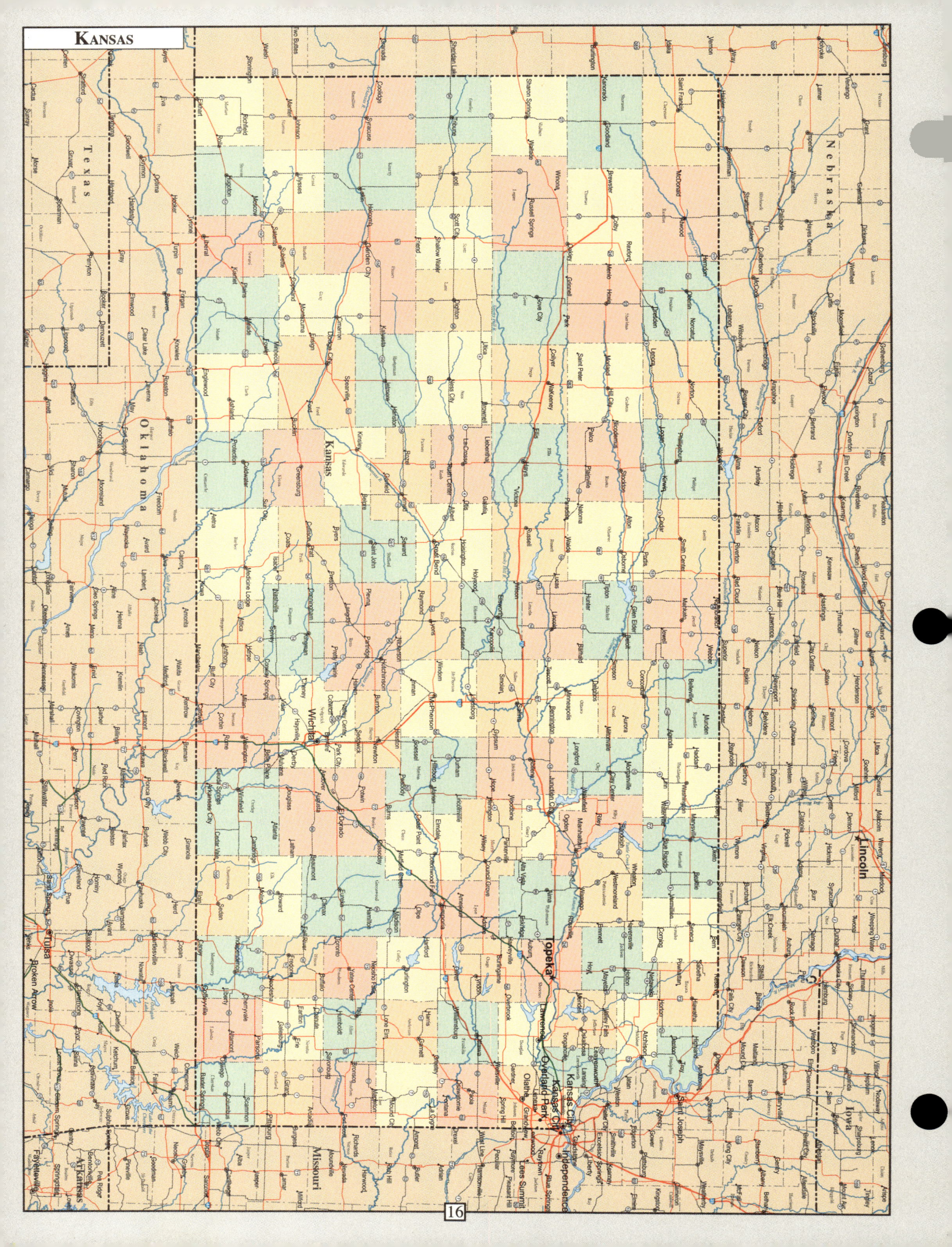

KENTUCKY

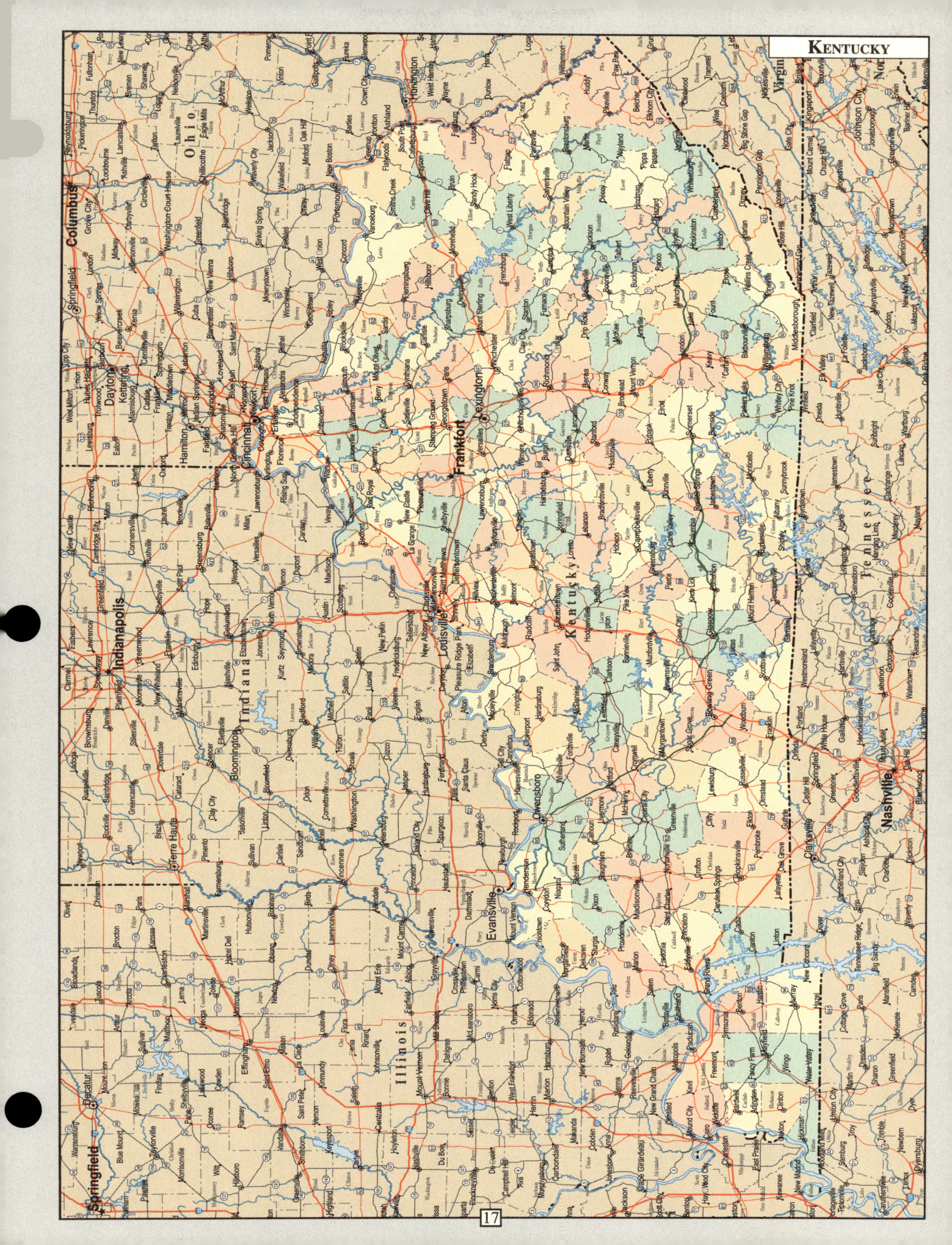

LOUISIANA

# MAINE

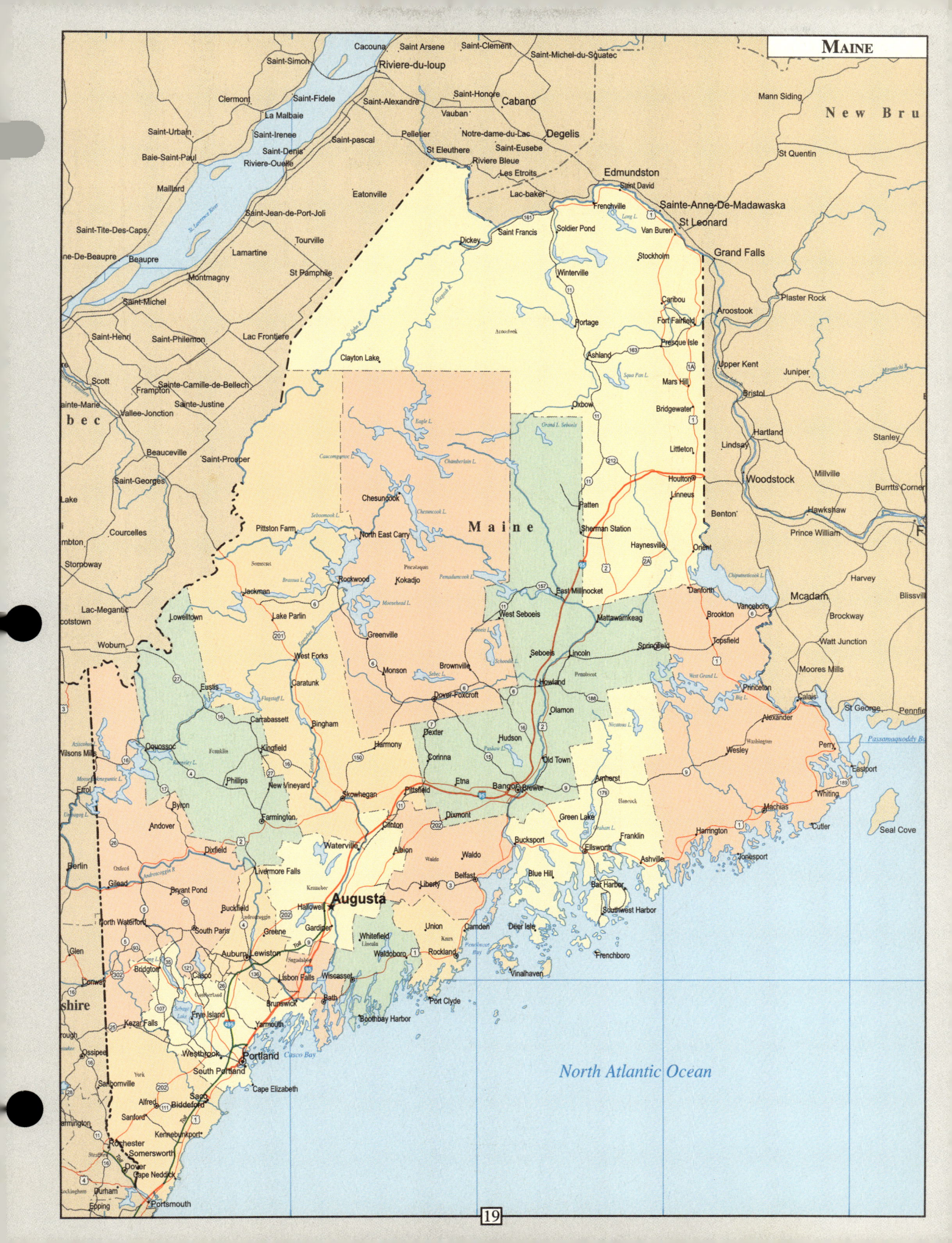

# MARYLAND

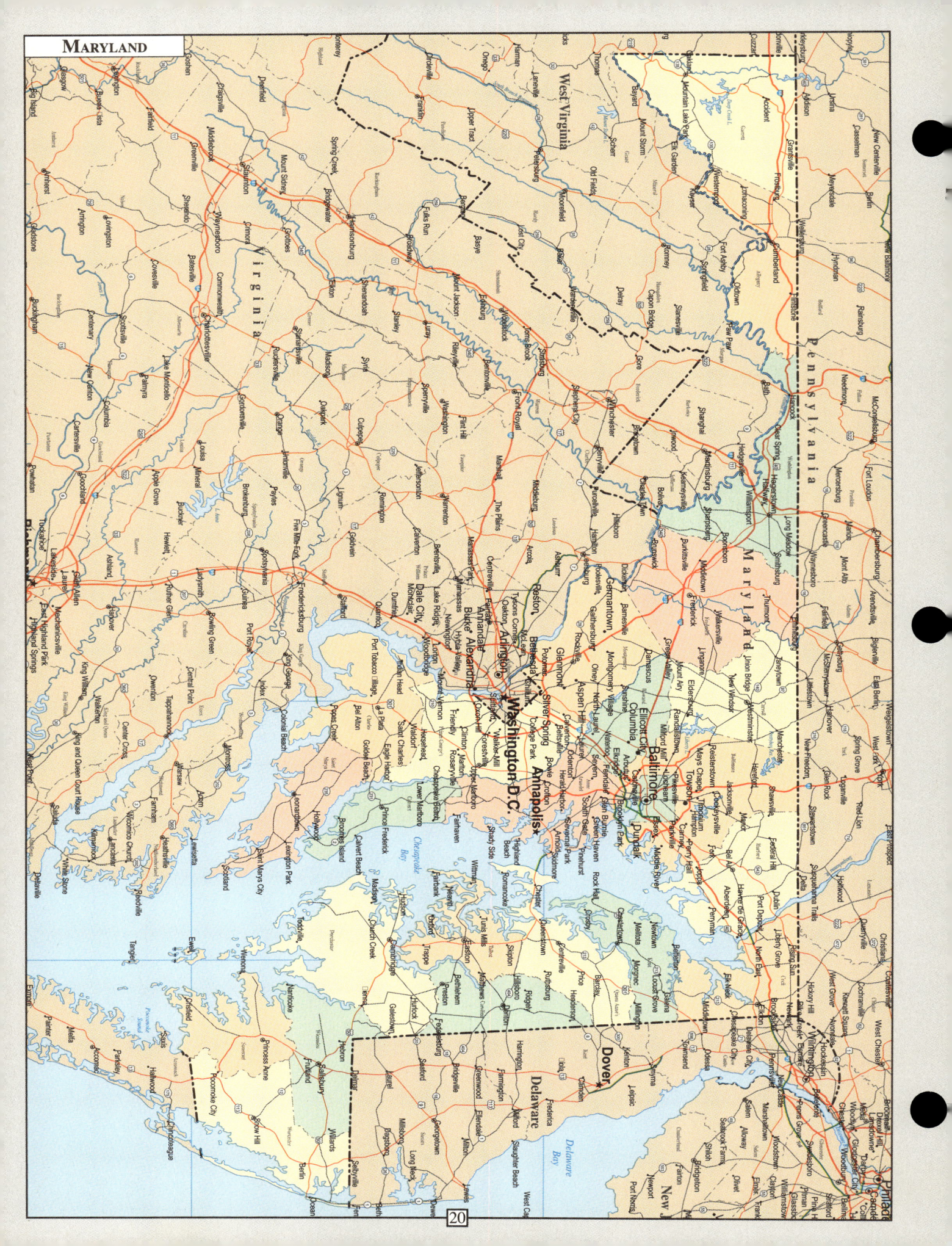

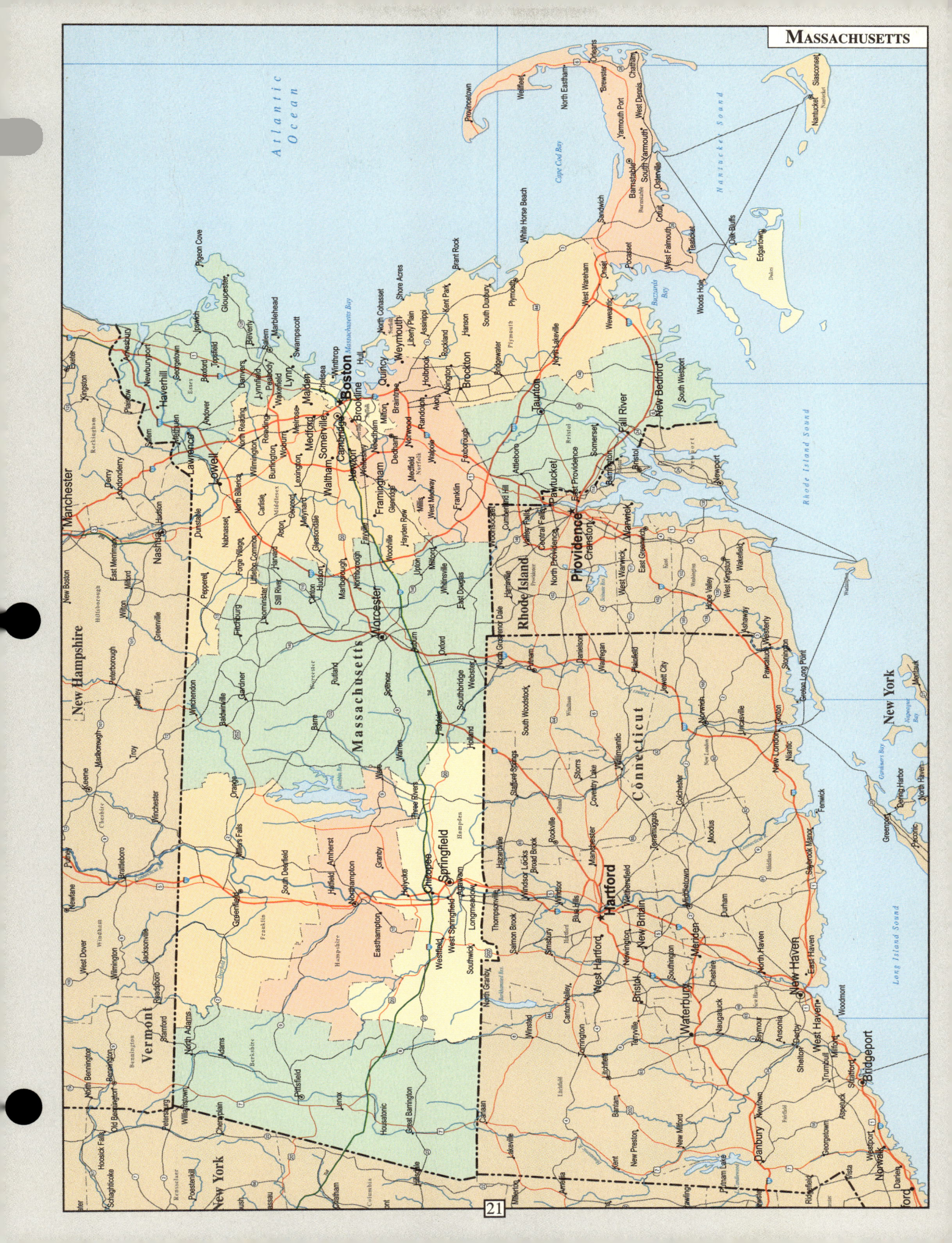

MASSACHUSETTS

# MICHIGAN

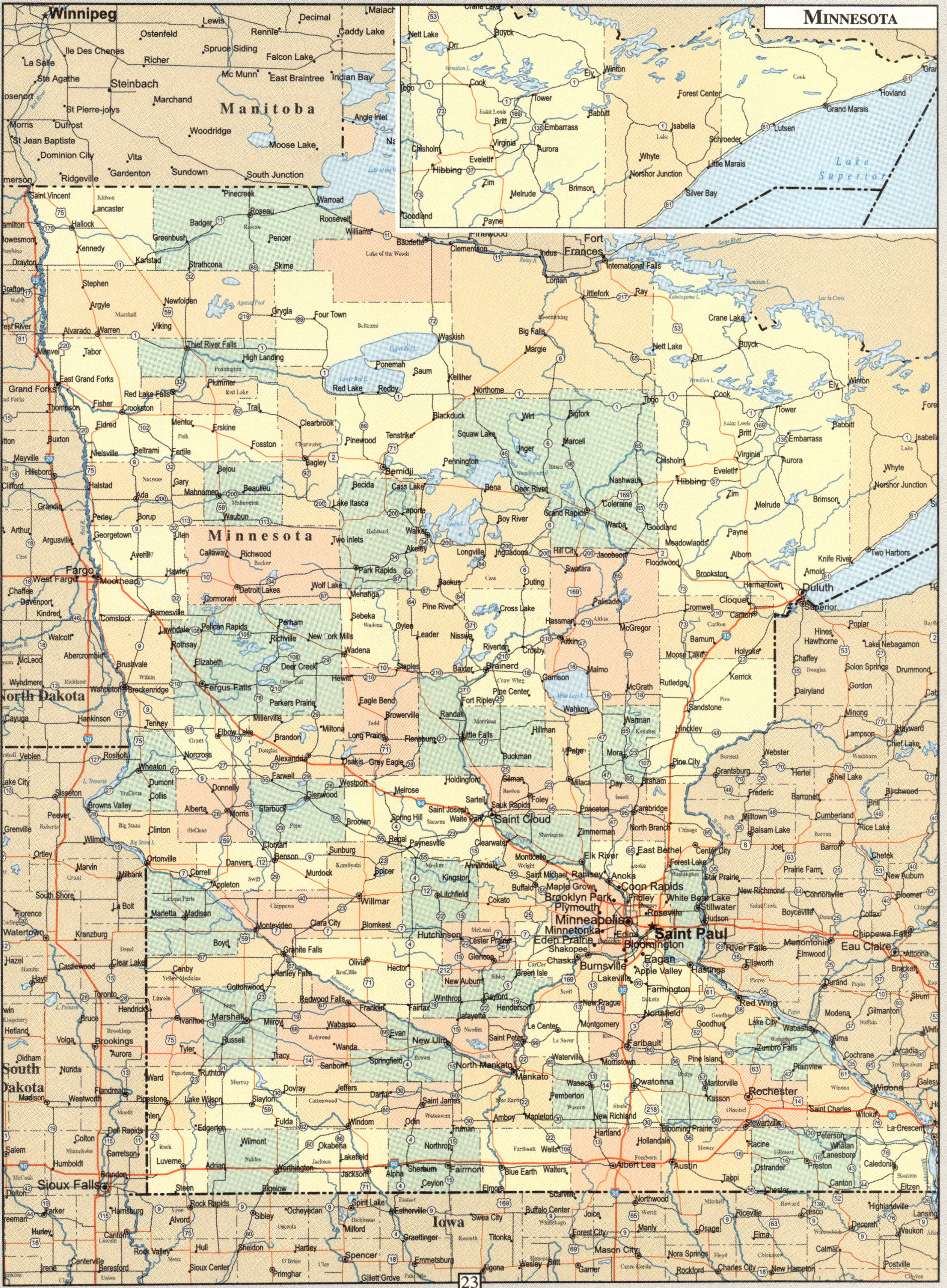

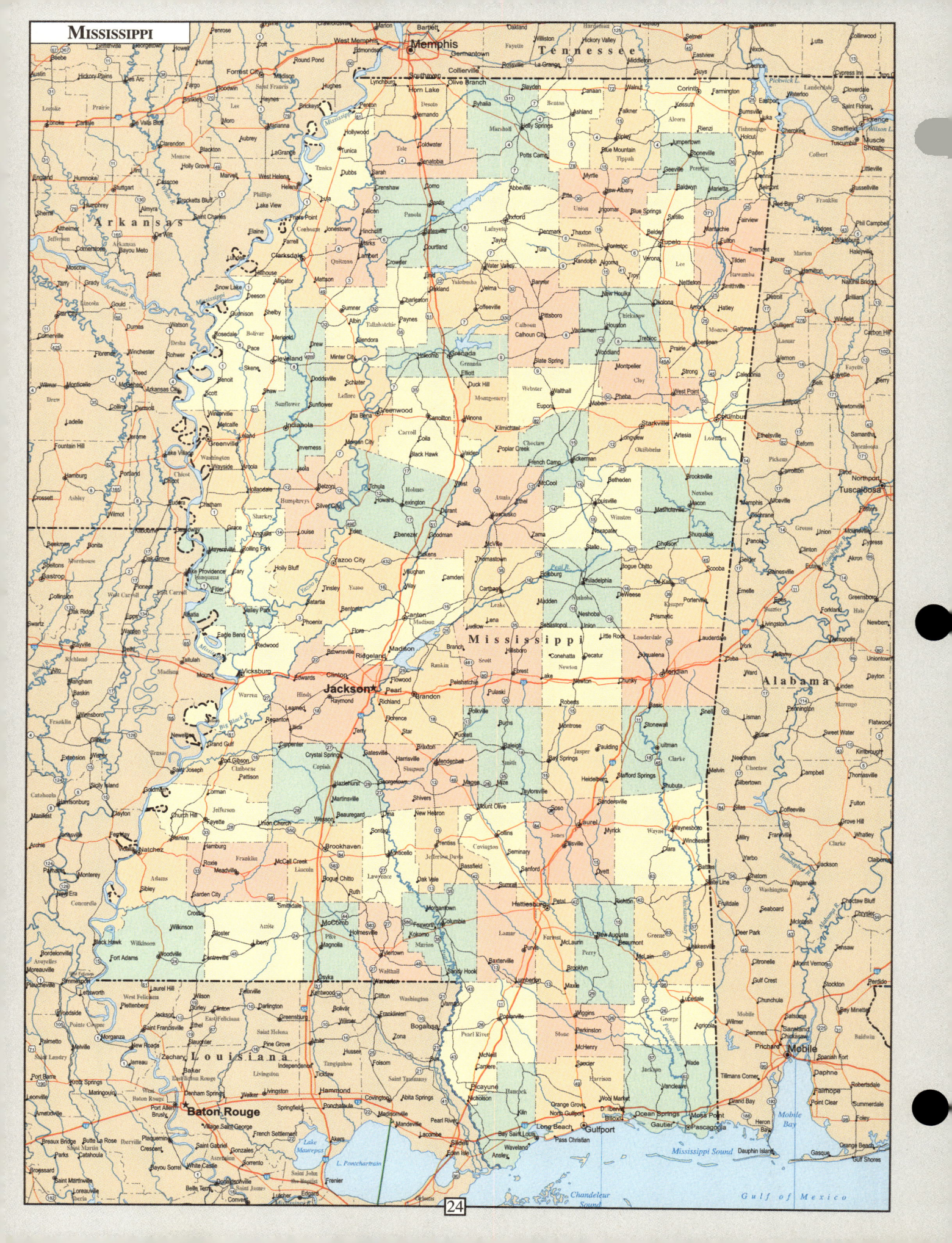

# MISSISSIPPI

**MISSOURI**

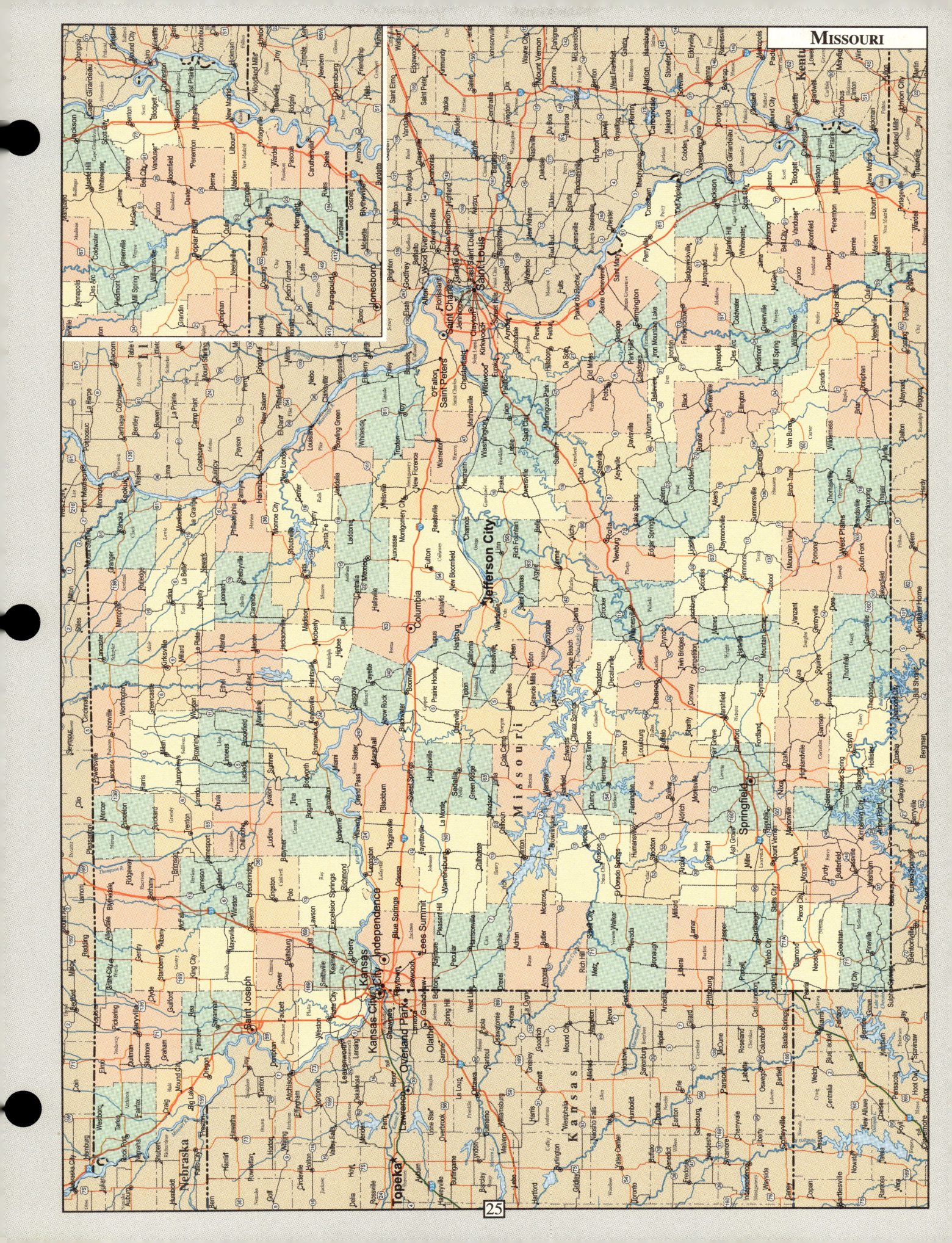

25

# Montana - Eastern

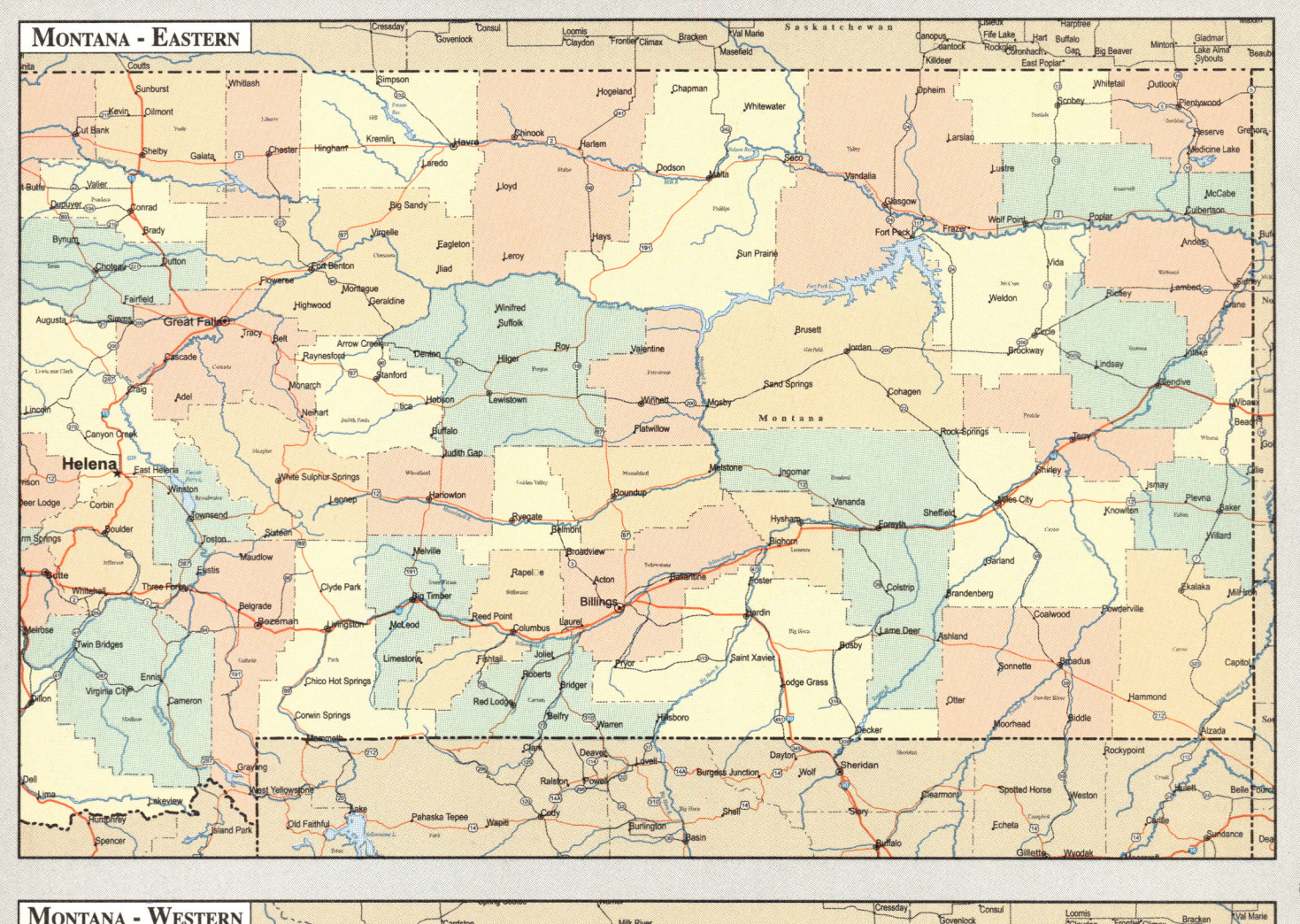

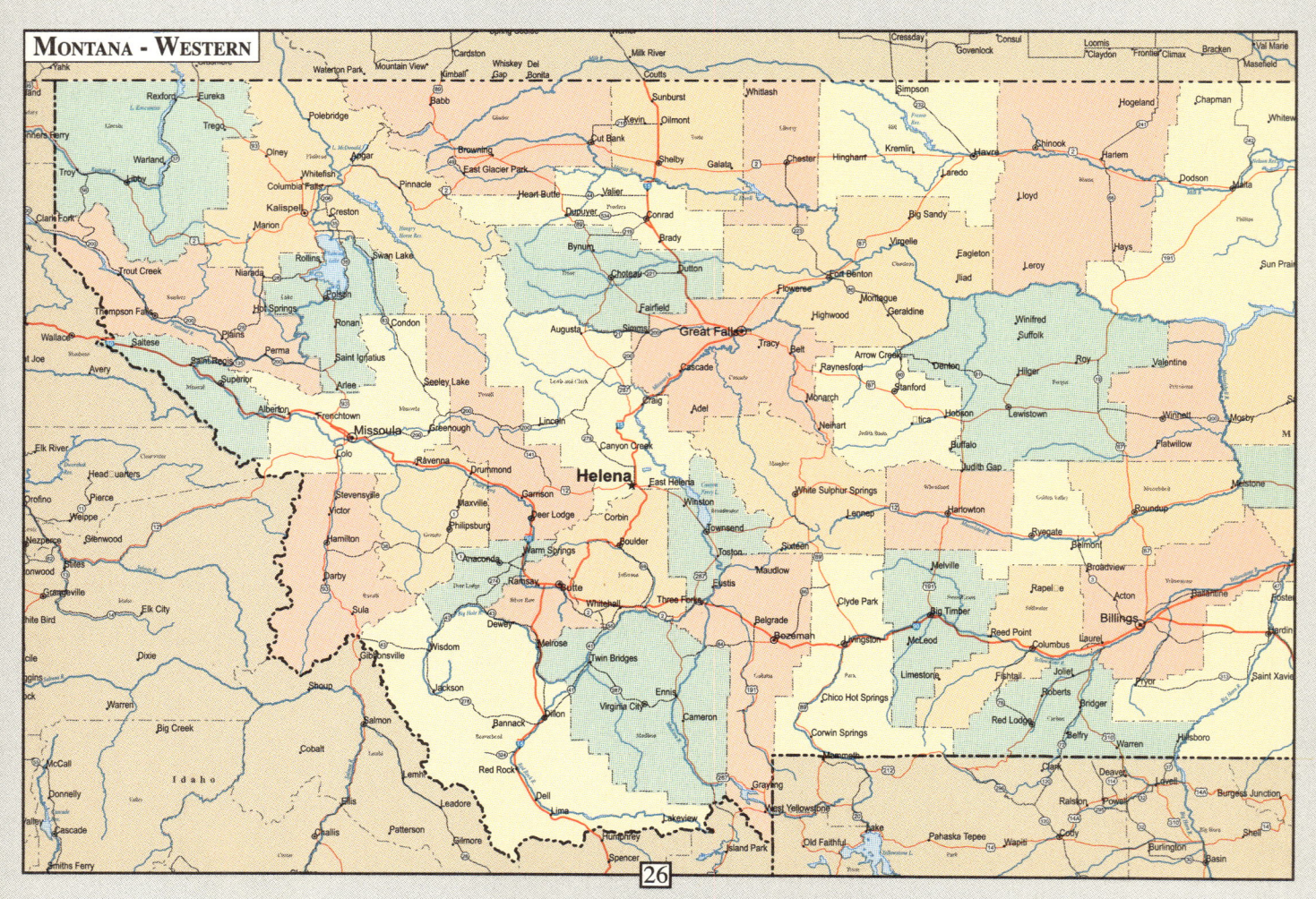

# Montana - Western

**Nebraska**

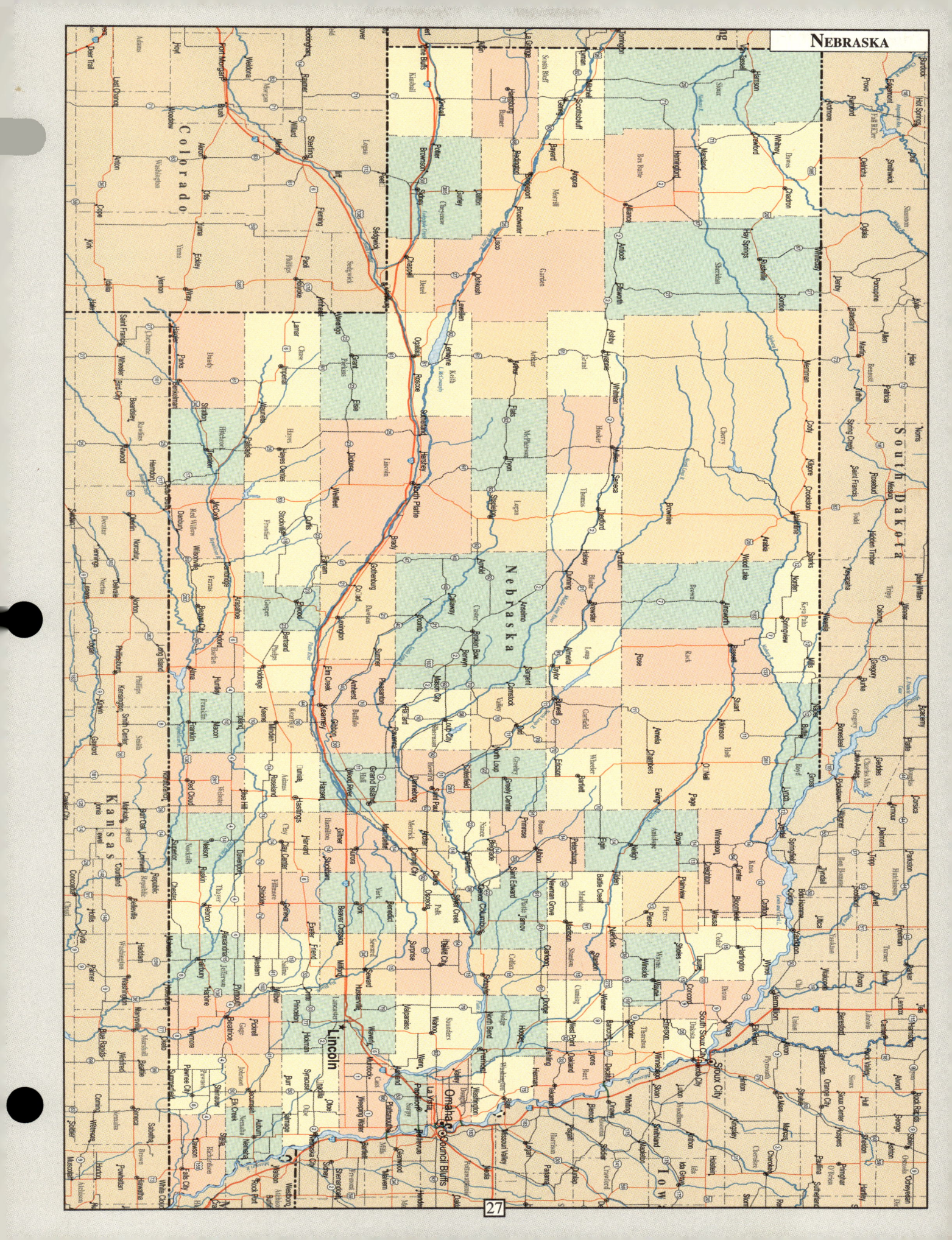

# NEVADA

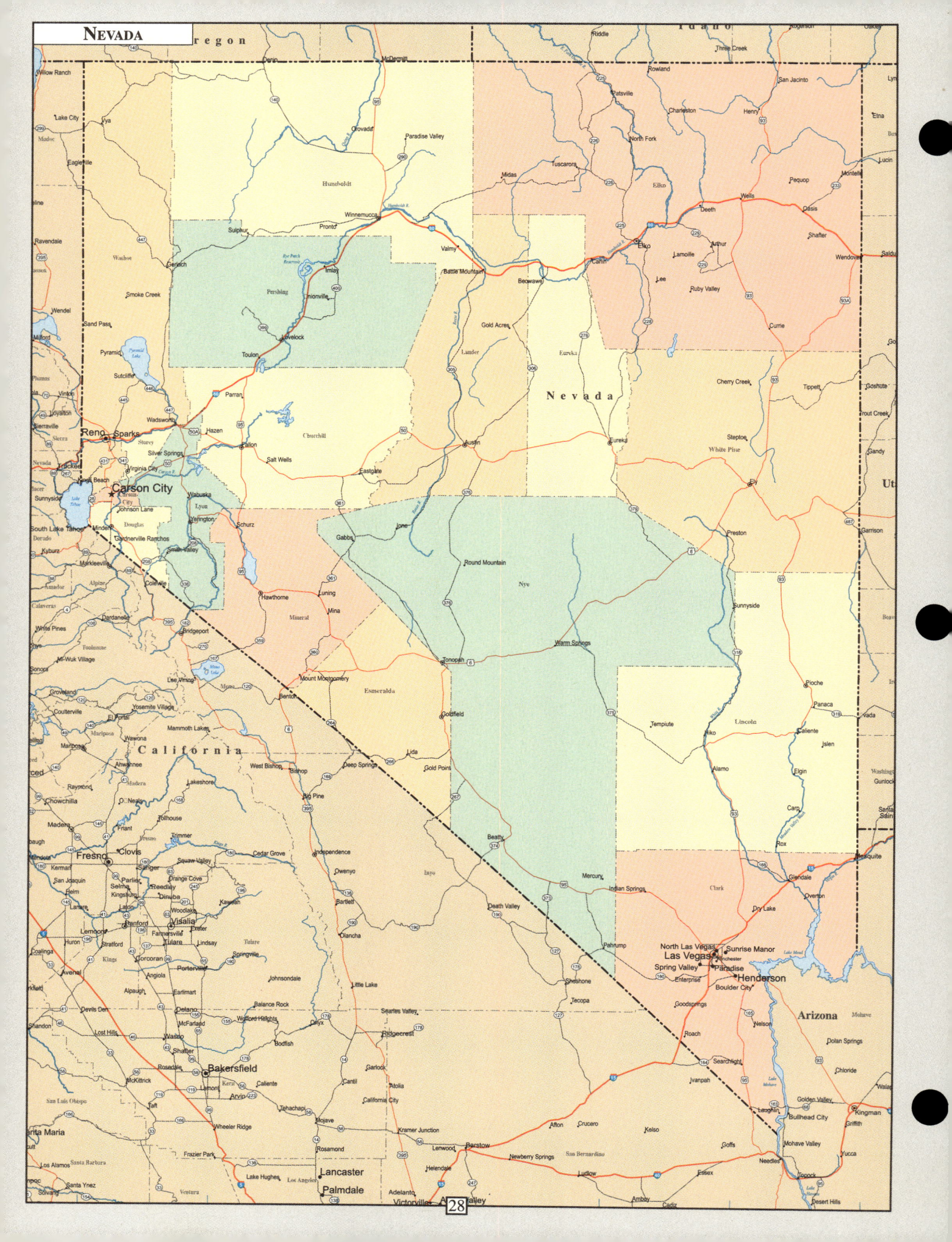

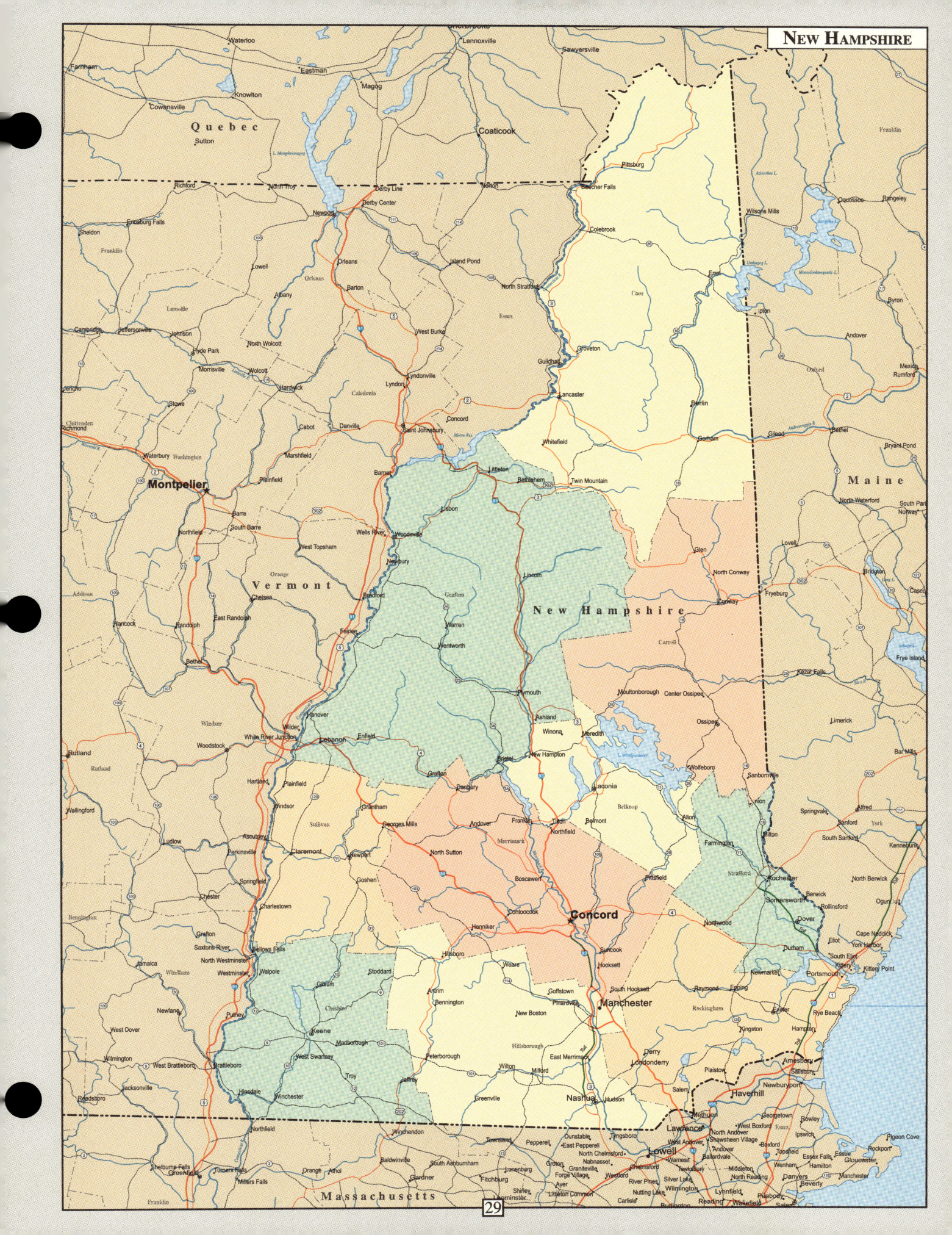

# New Hampshire

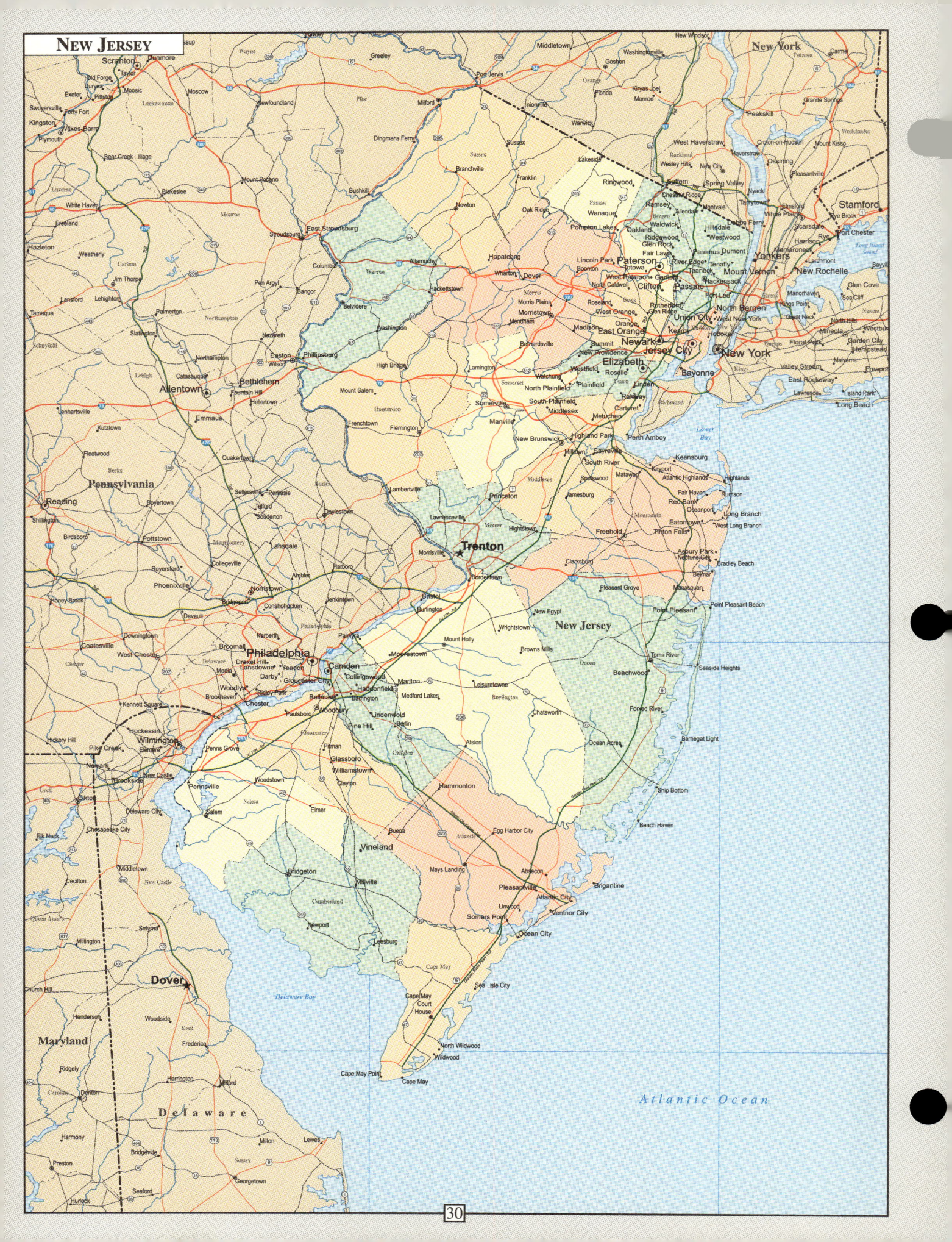

# NEW JERSEY

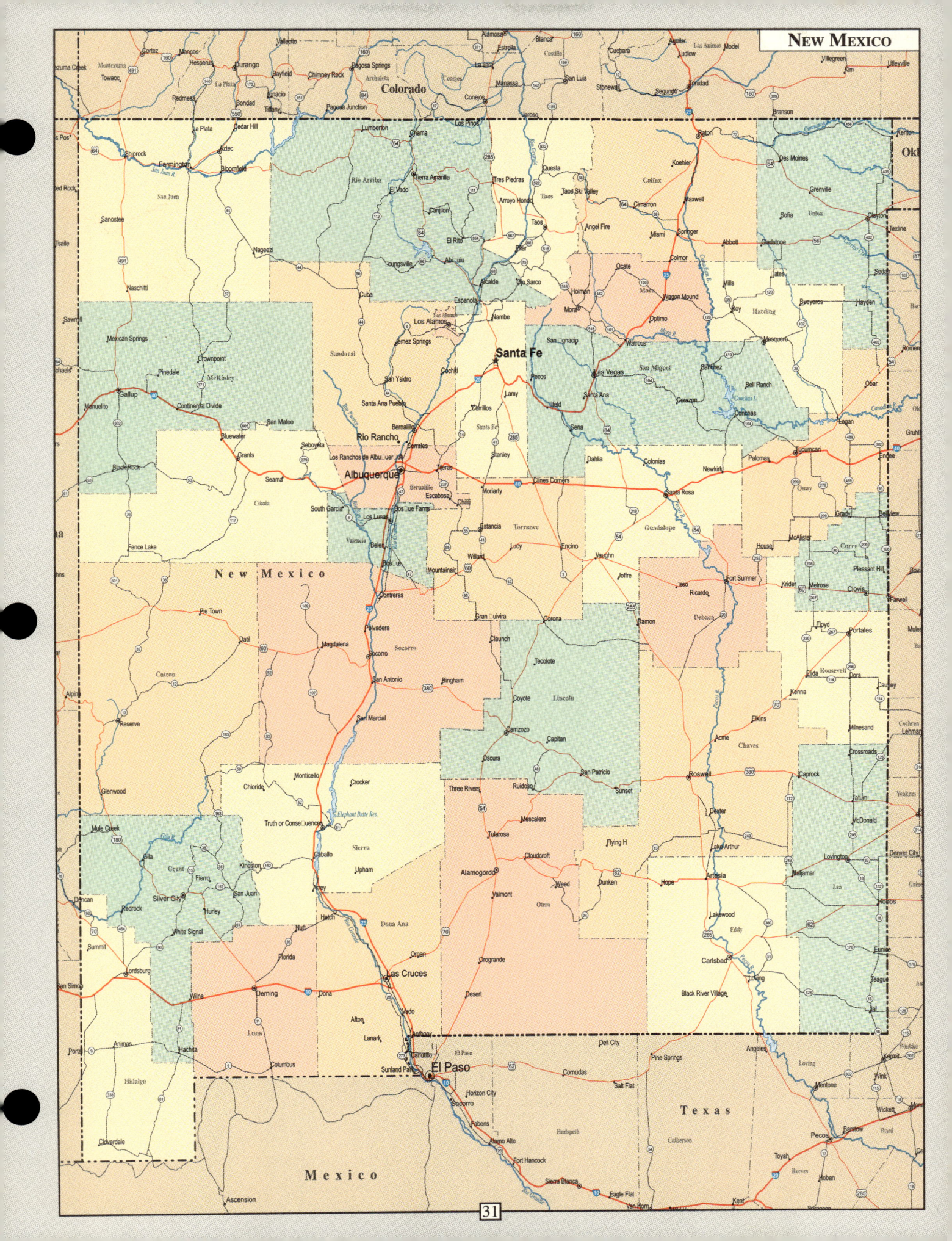

# NEW MEXICO

# New York

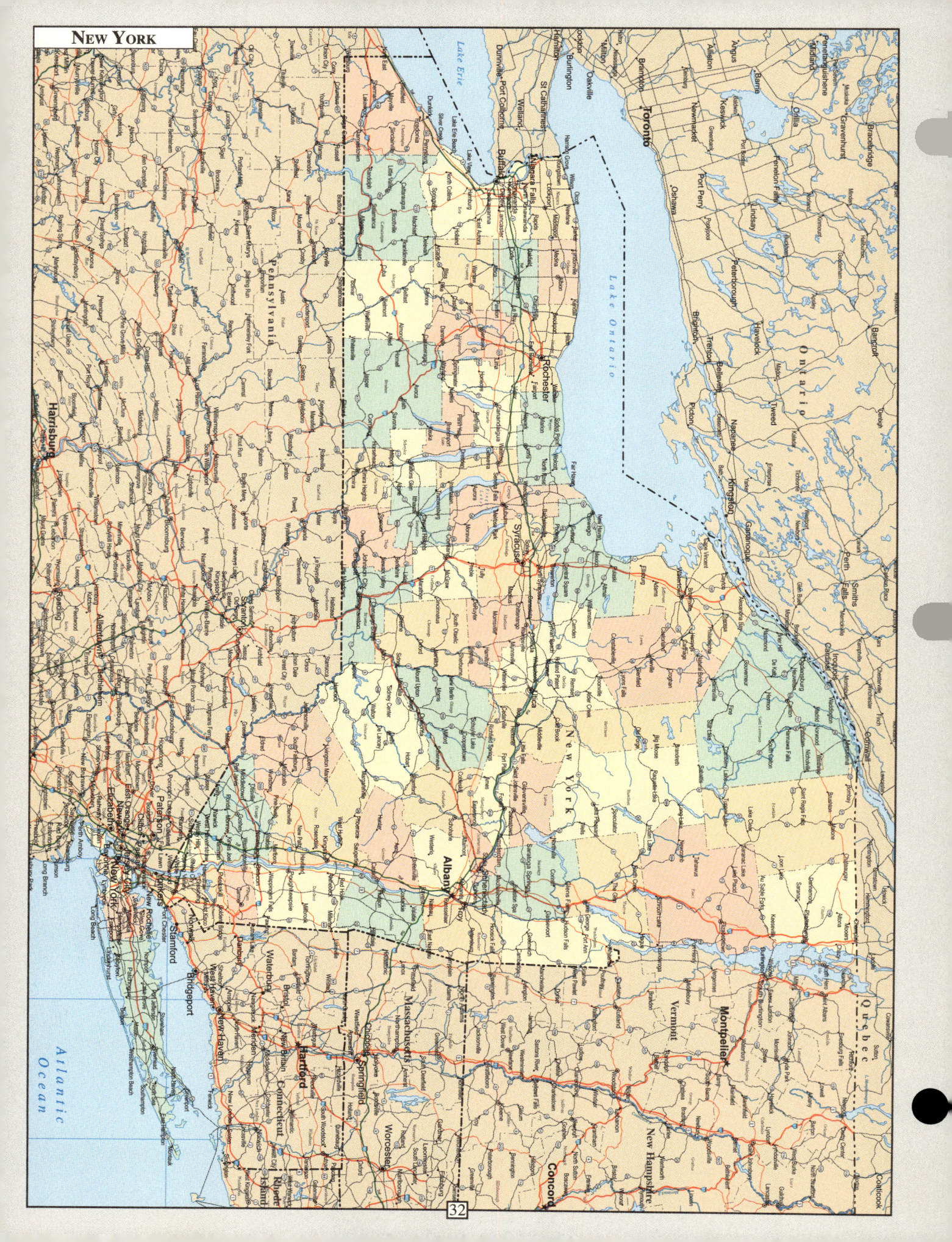

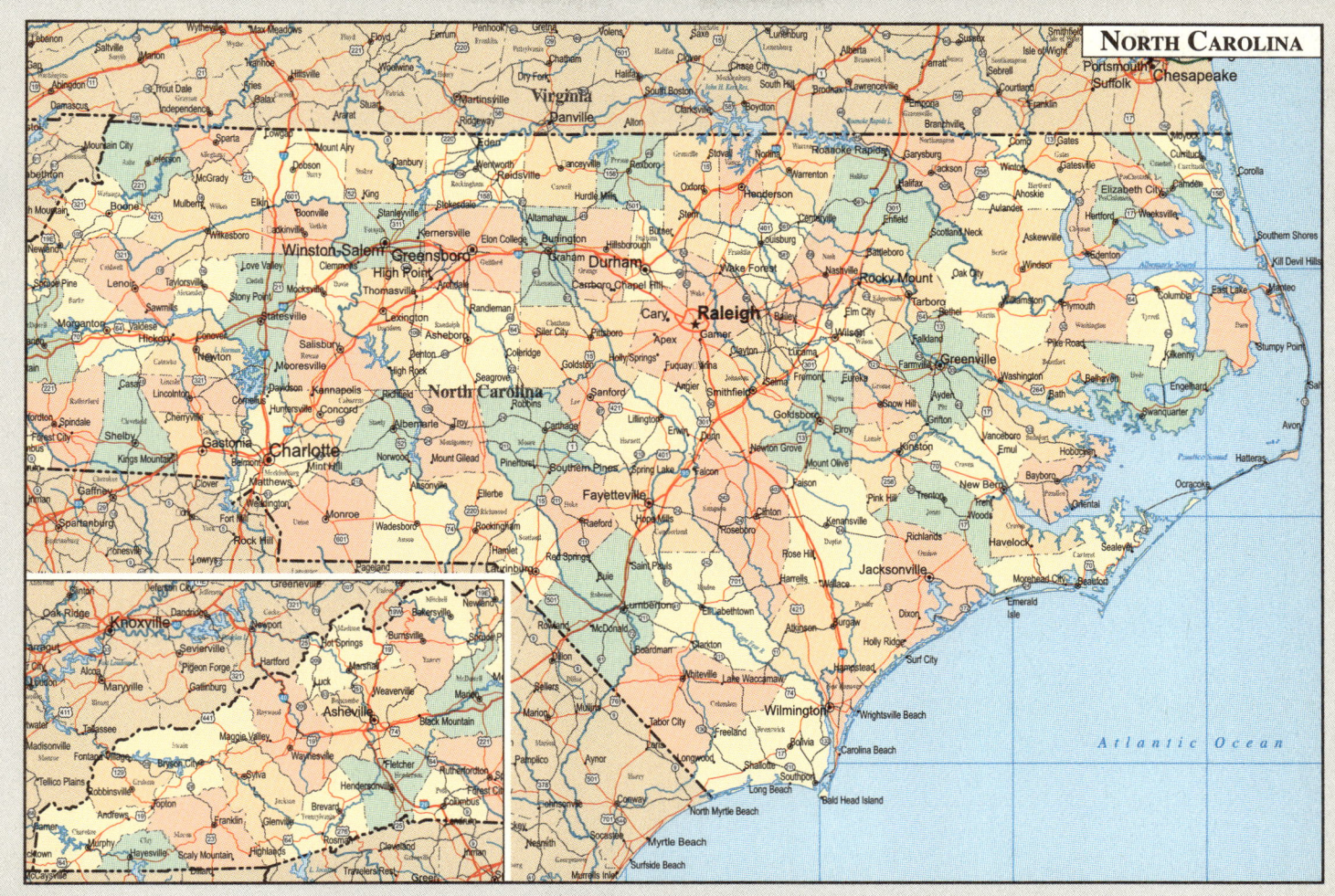

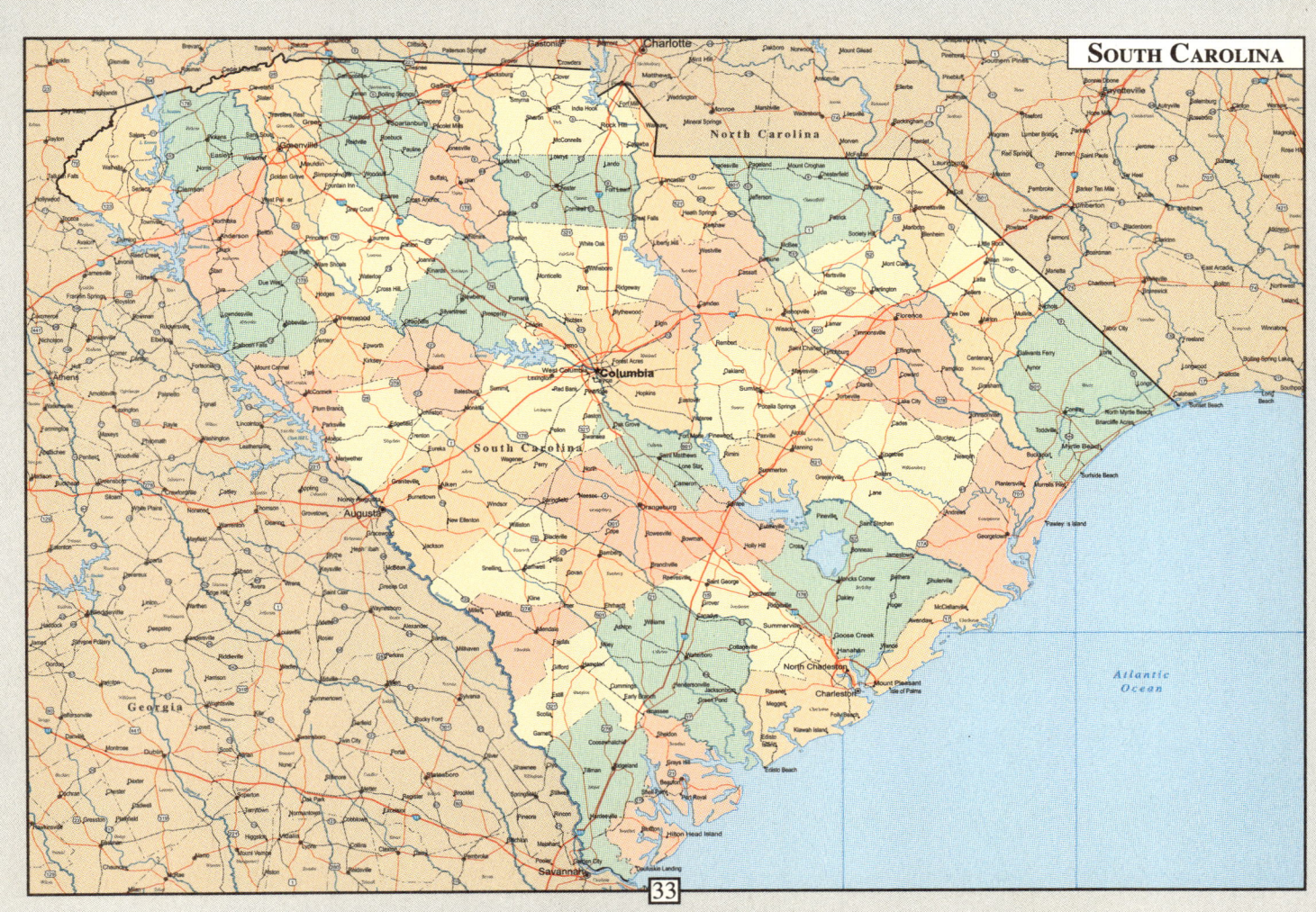

# NORTH CAROLINA

# SOUTH CAROLINA

# North Dakota

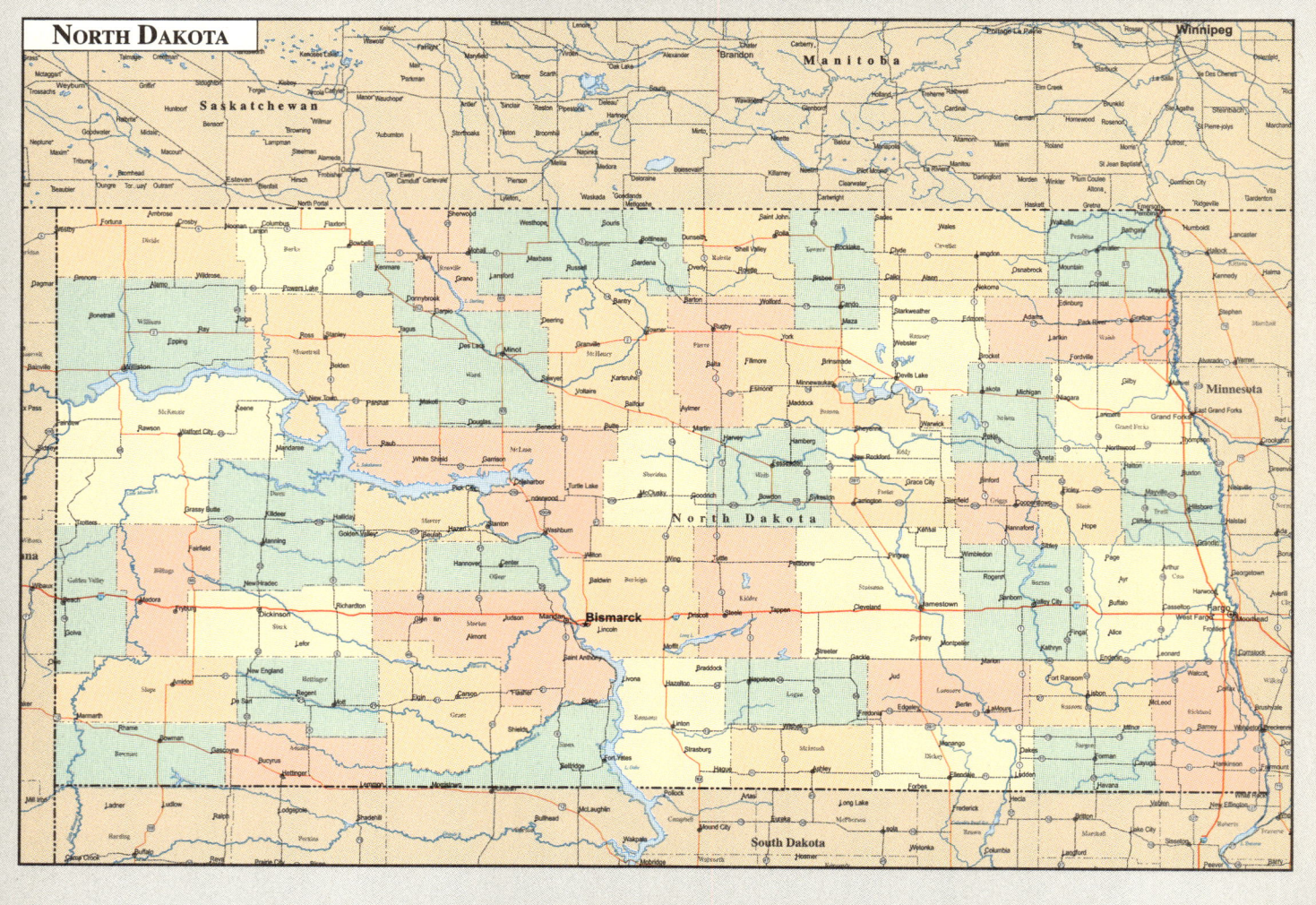

# South Dakota

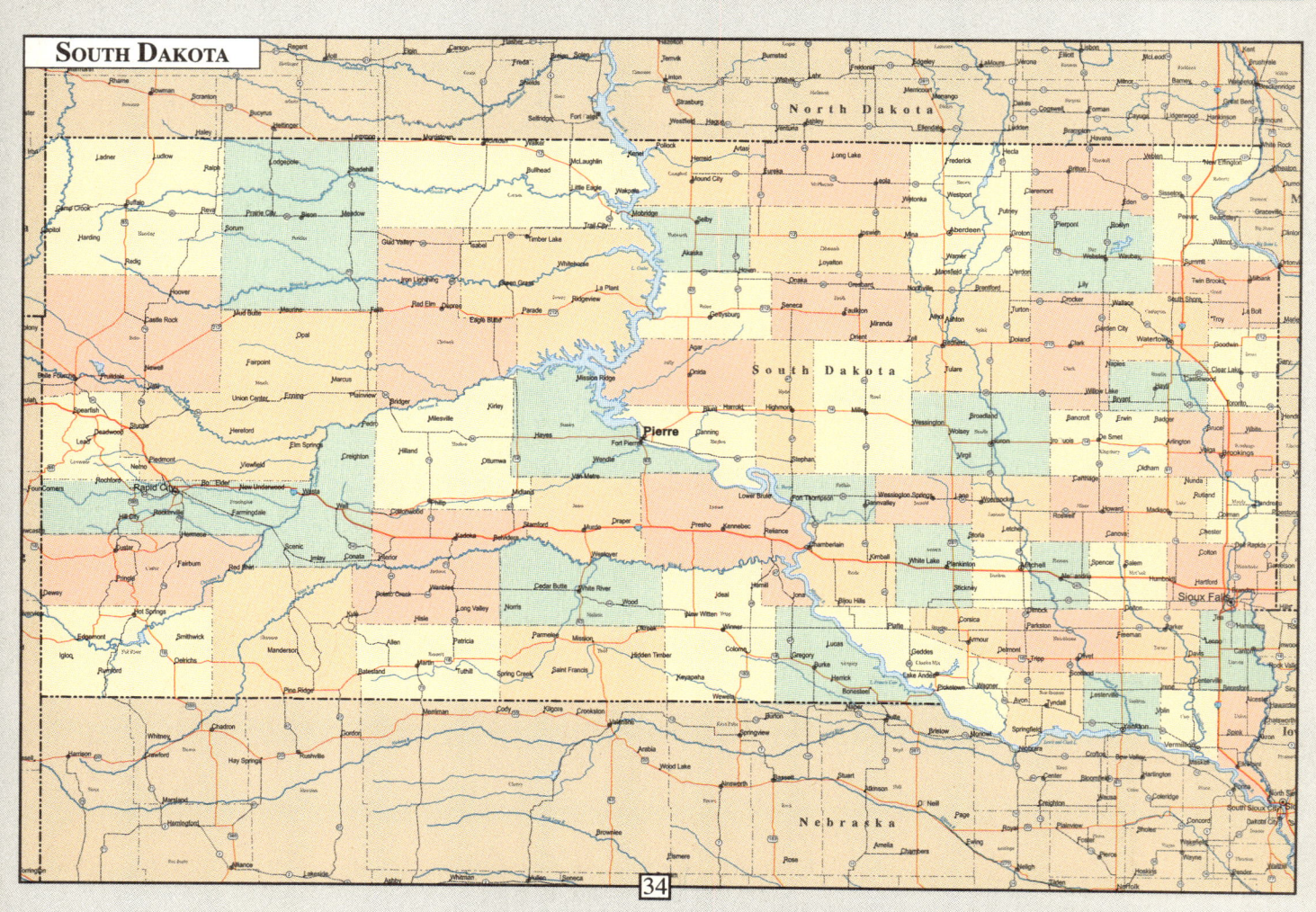

Ohio

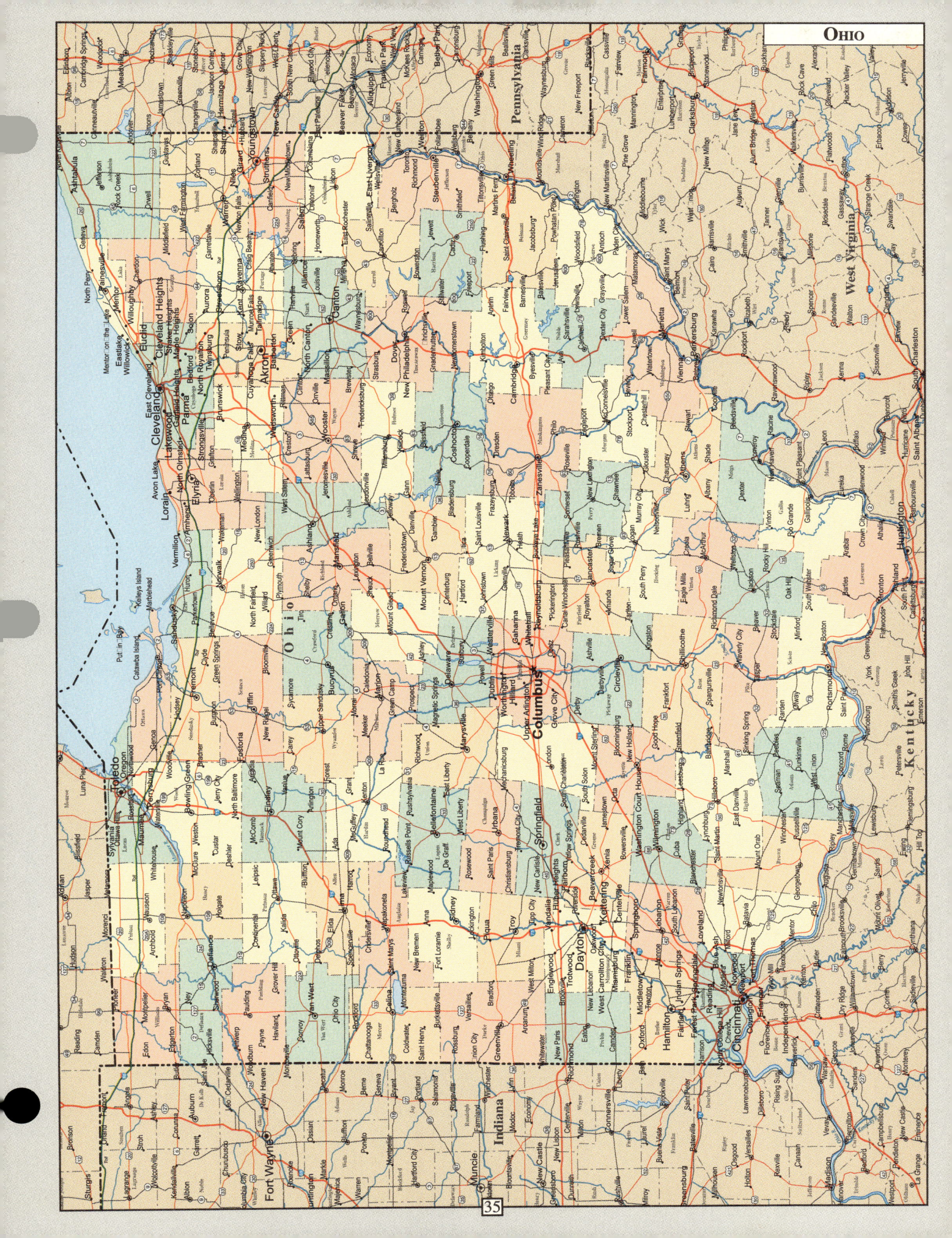

# OKLAHOMA

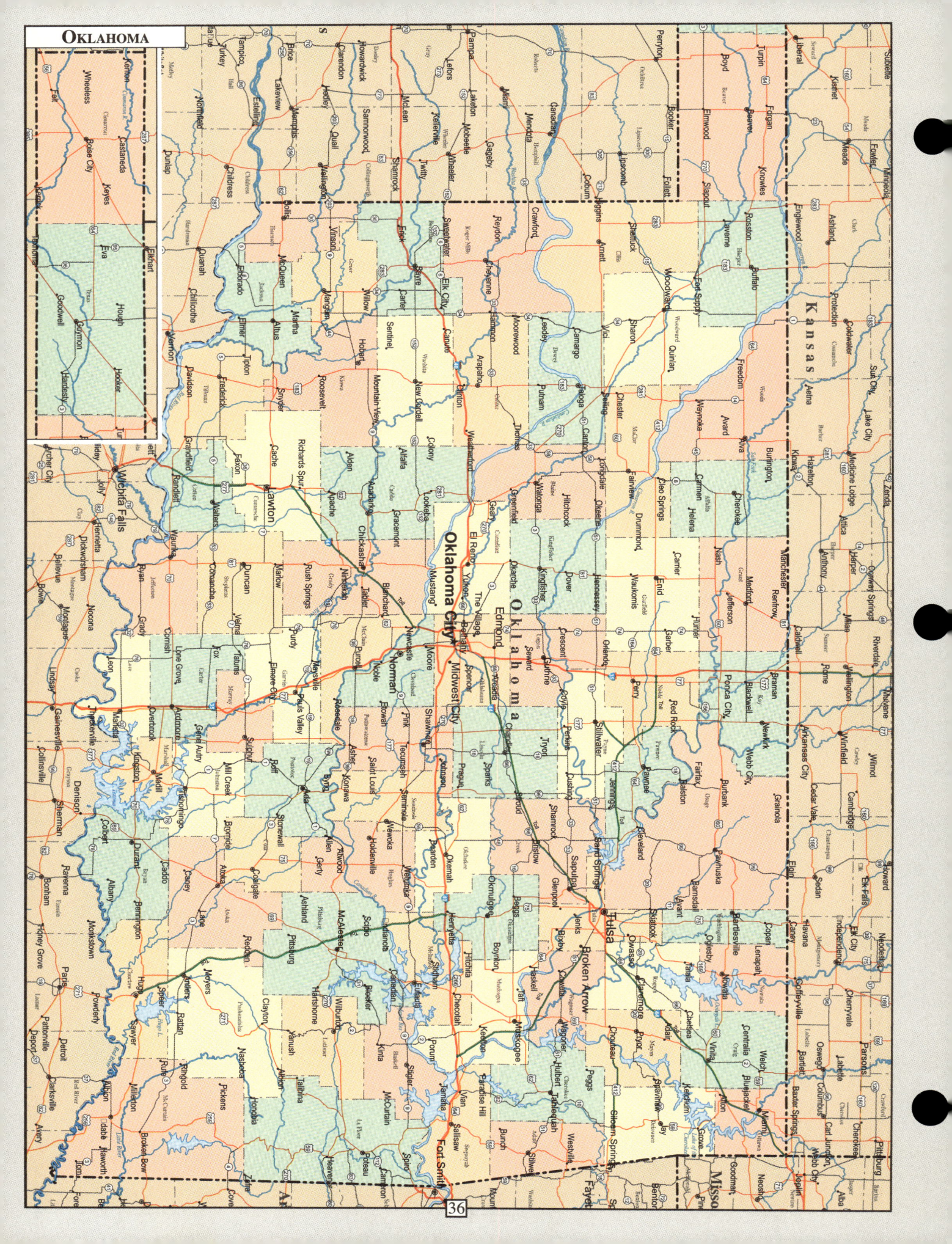

36

**OREGON**

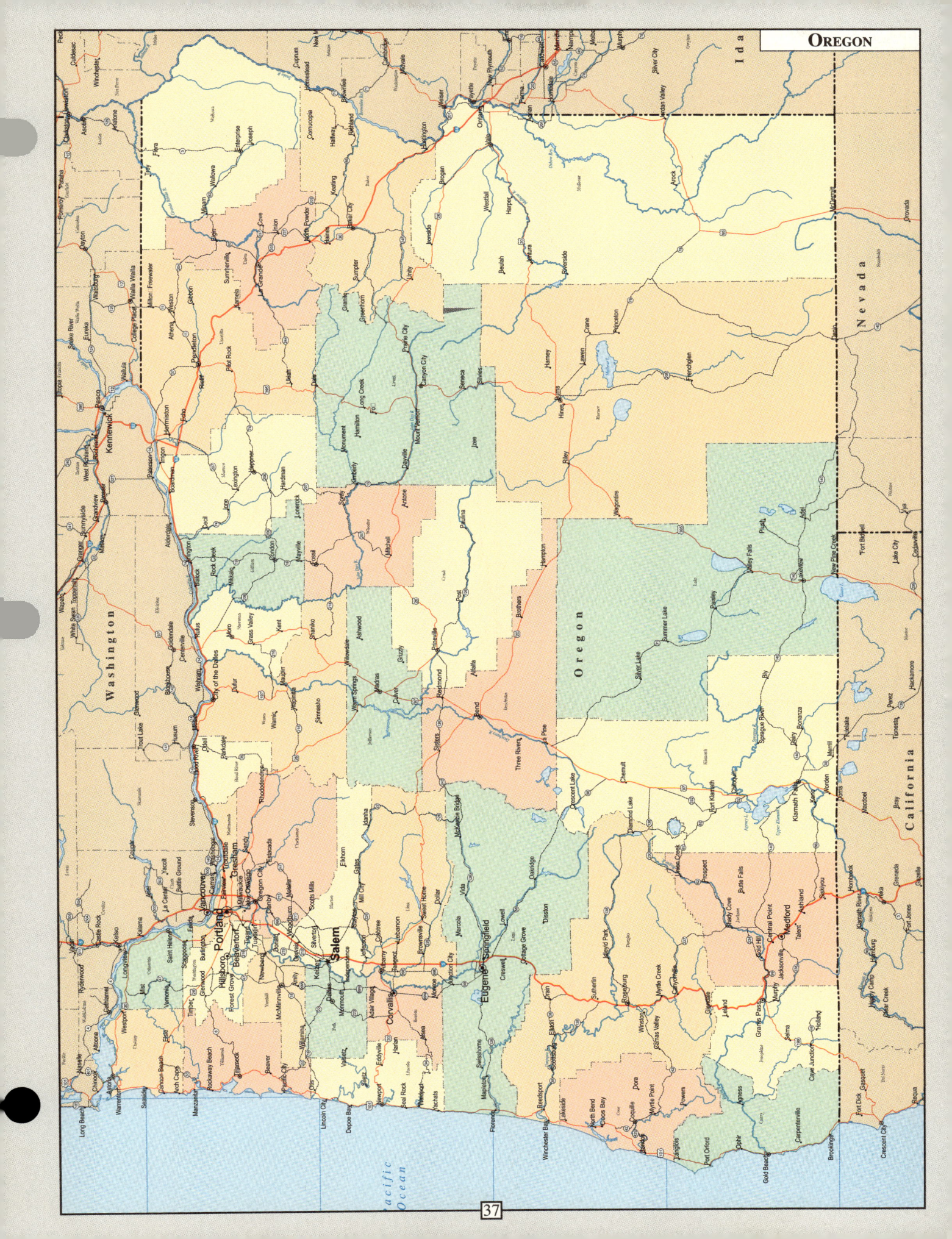

# PENNSYLVANIA - EASTERN

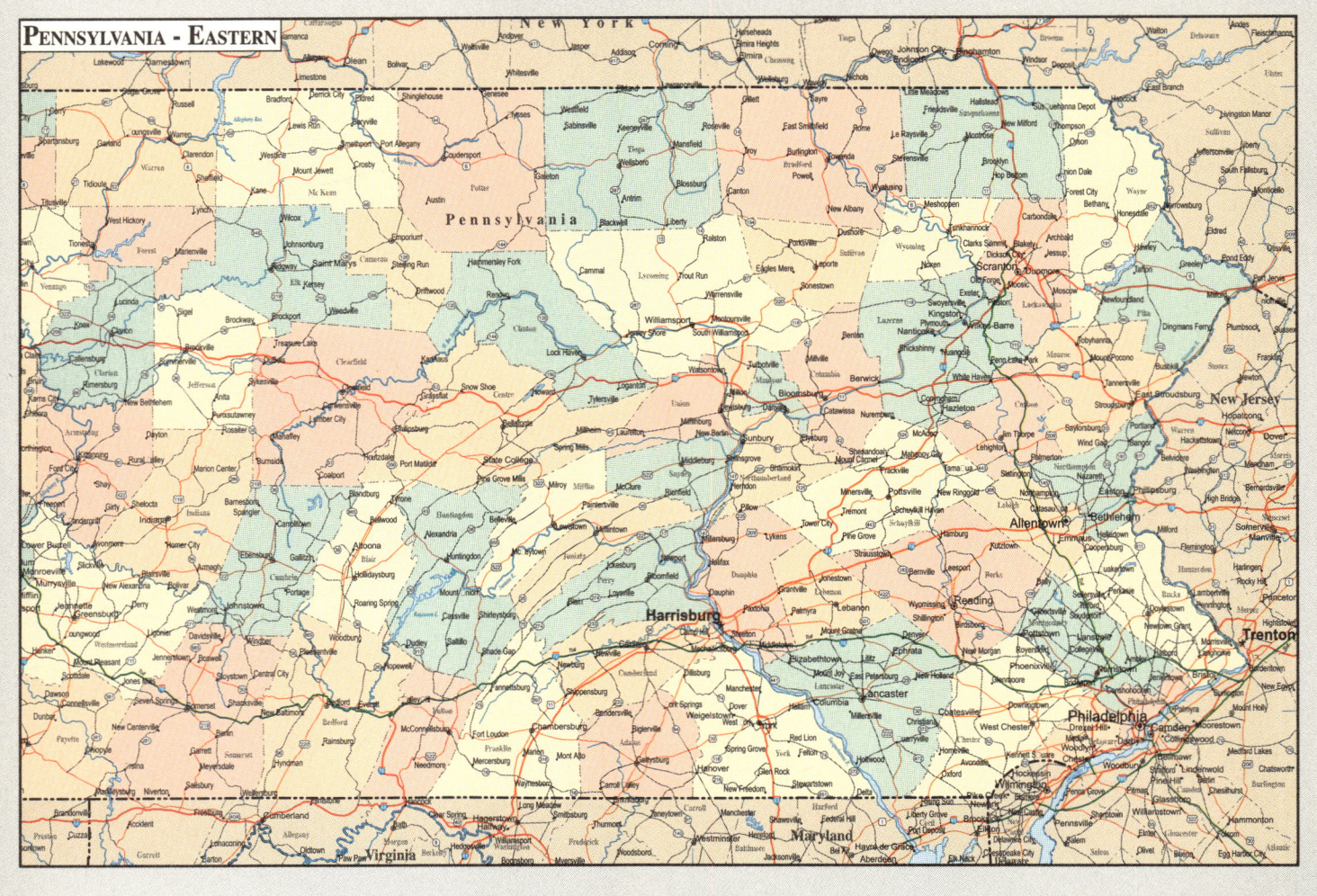

# PENNSYLVANIA - WESTERN

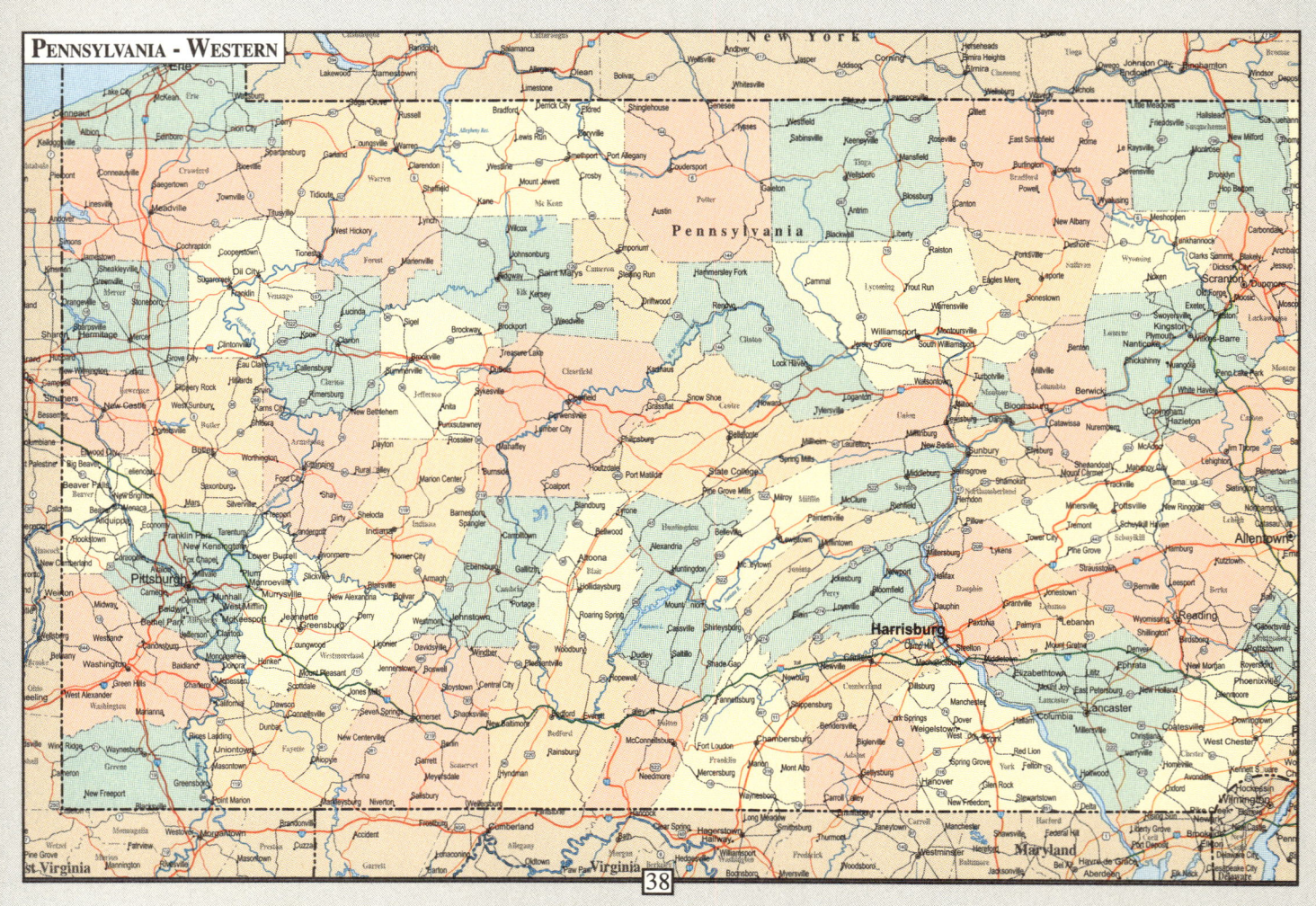

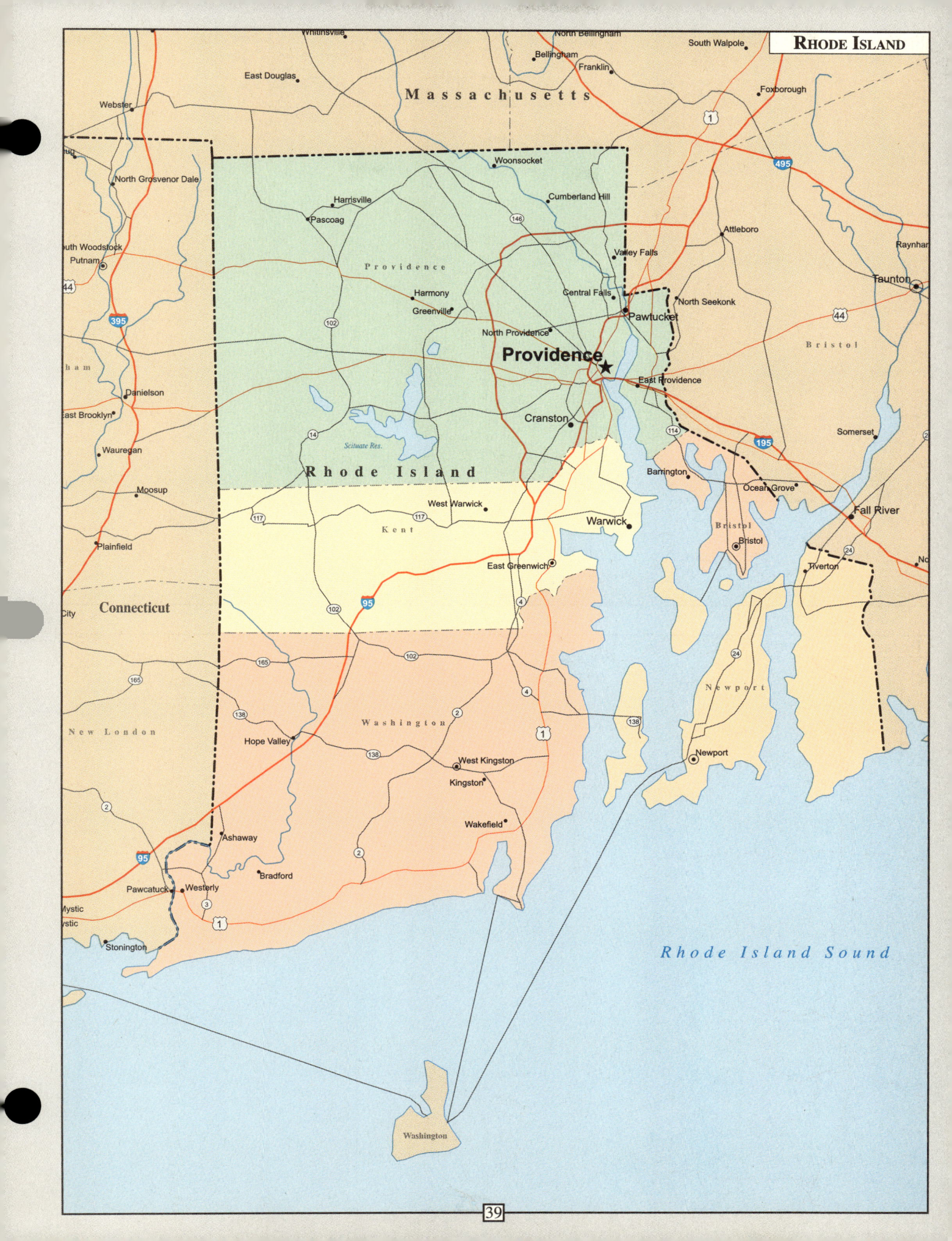

# Rhode Island

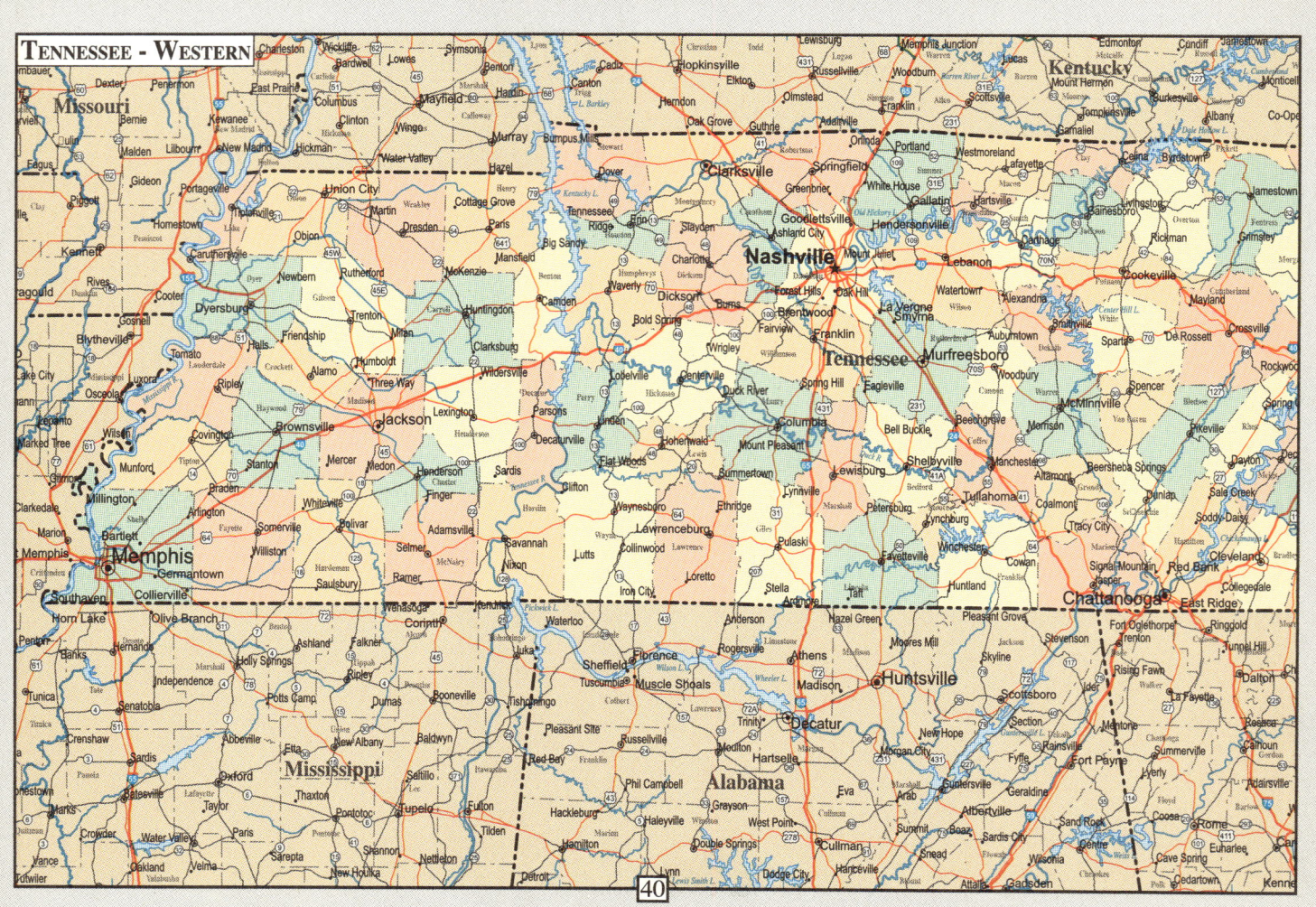

**TENNESSEE - EASTERN**

**TENNESSEE - WESTERN**

# Texas

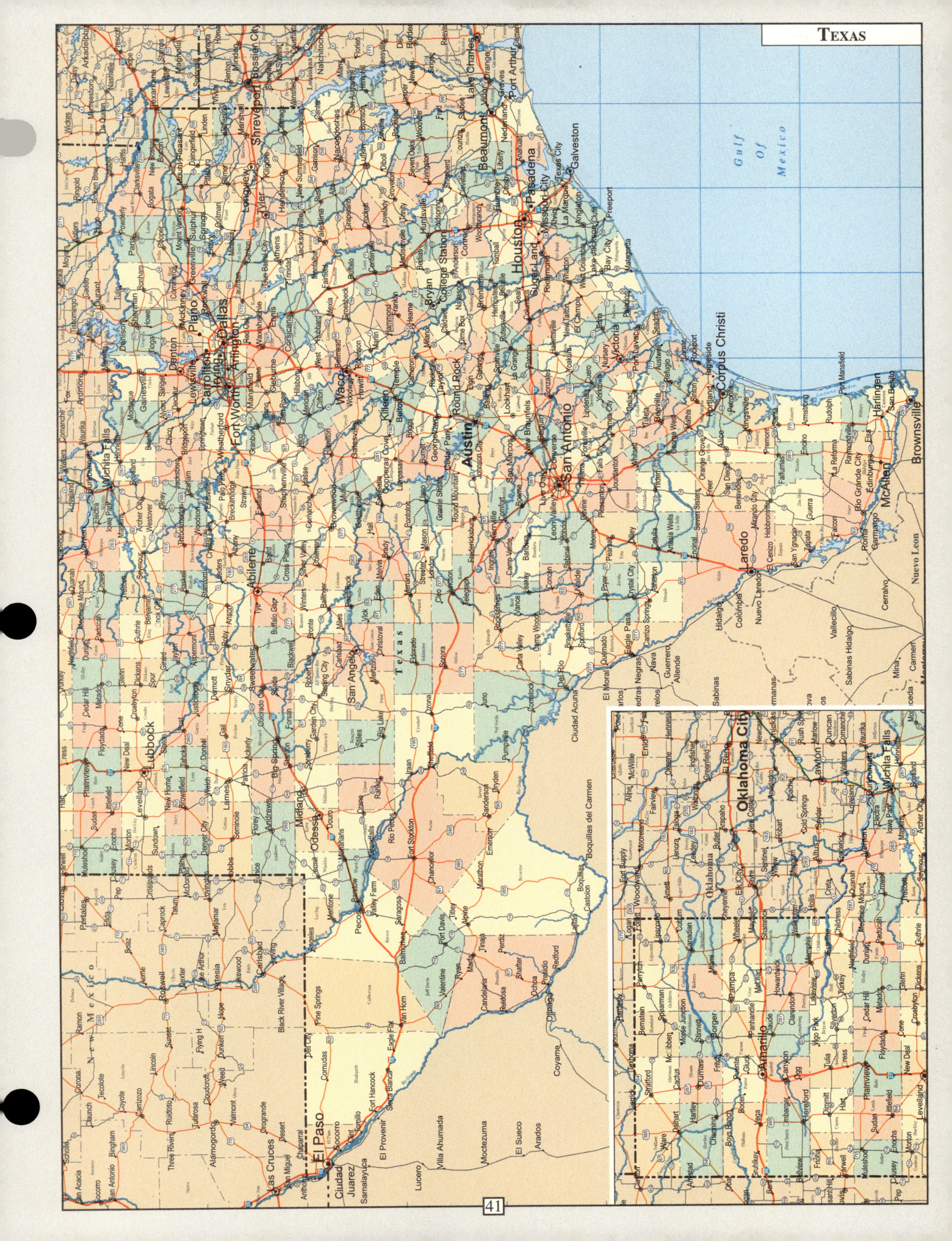

# UTAH

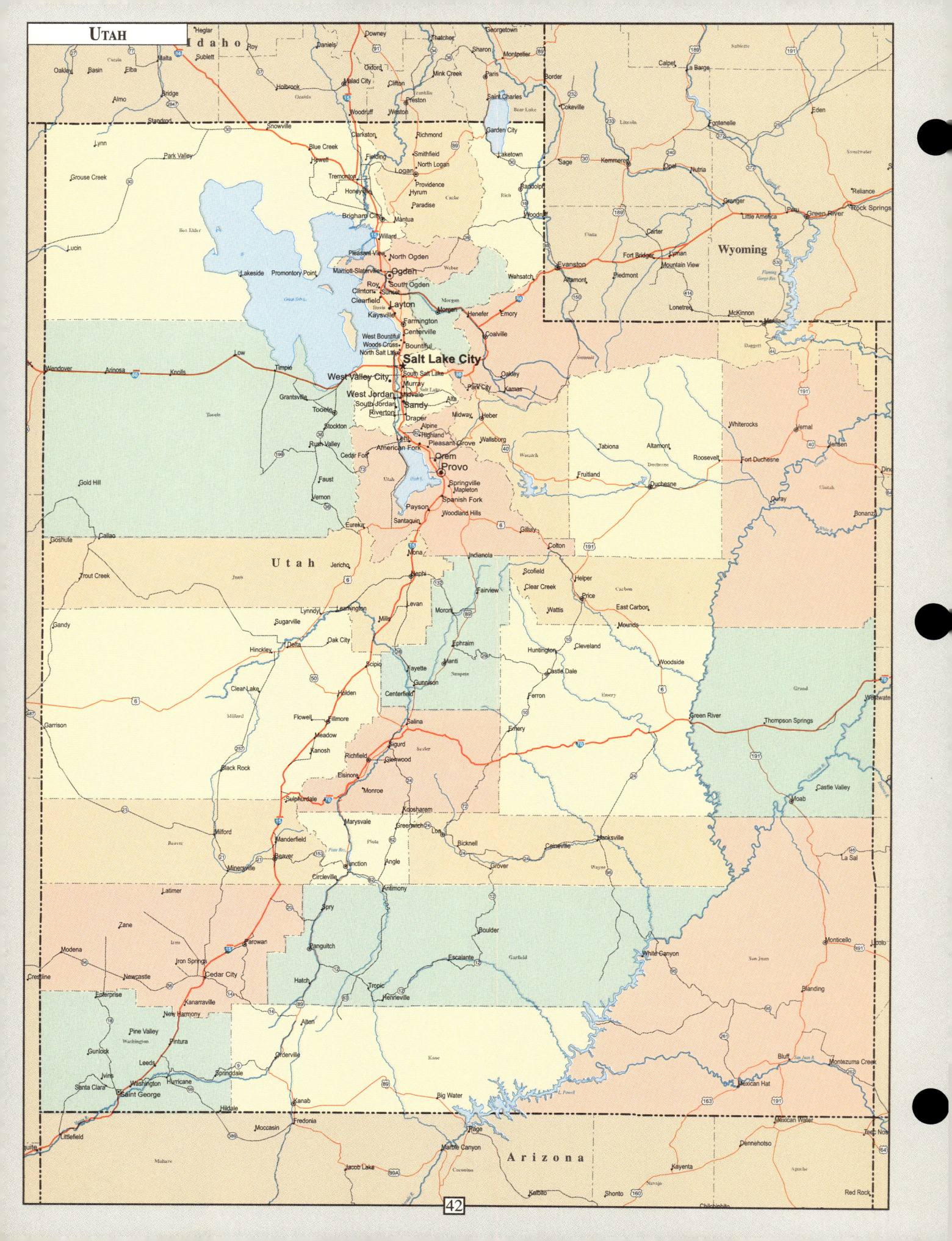

# Vermont

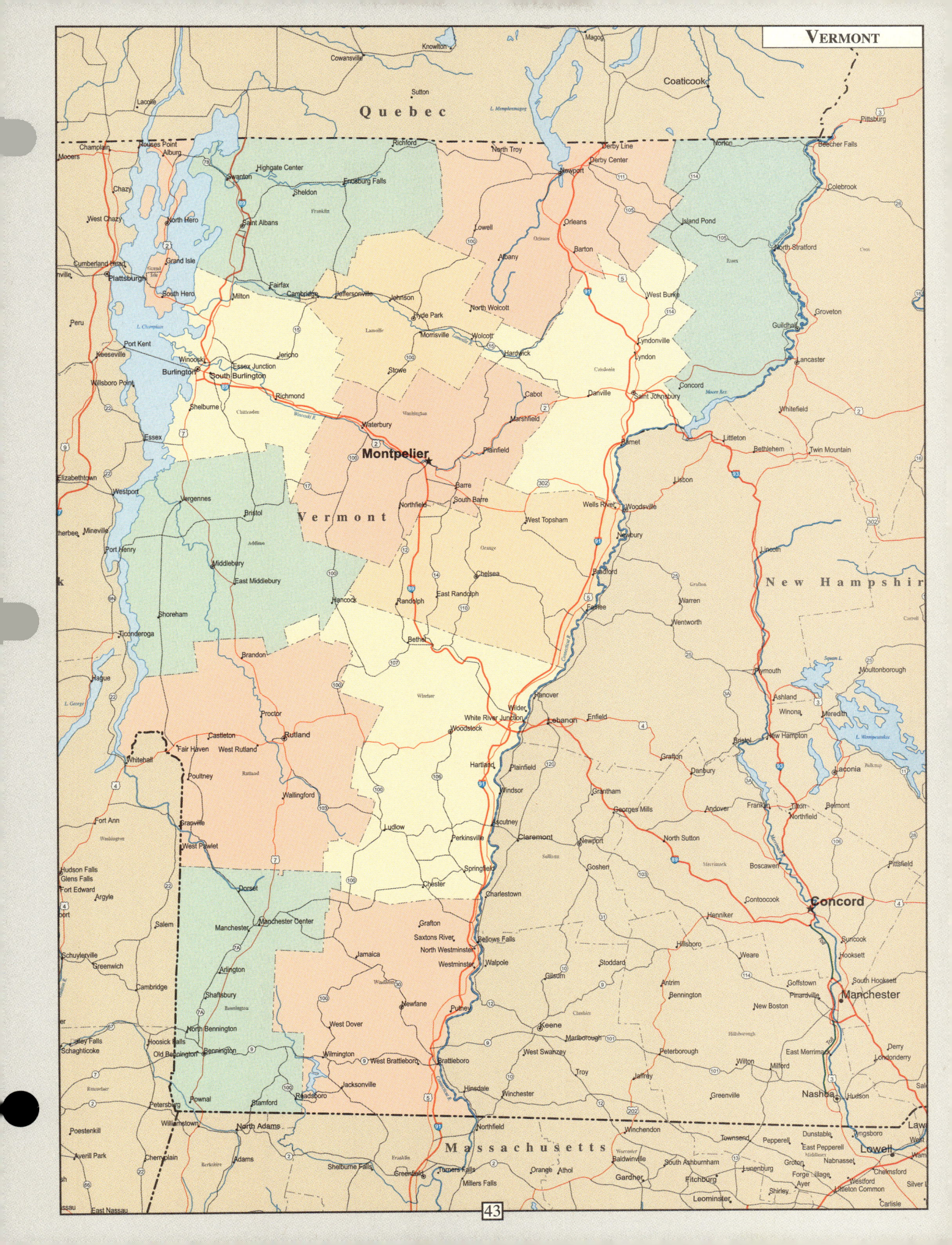

# Virginia

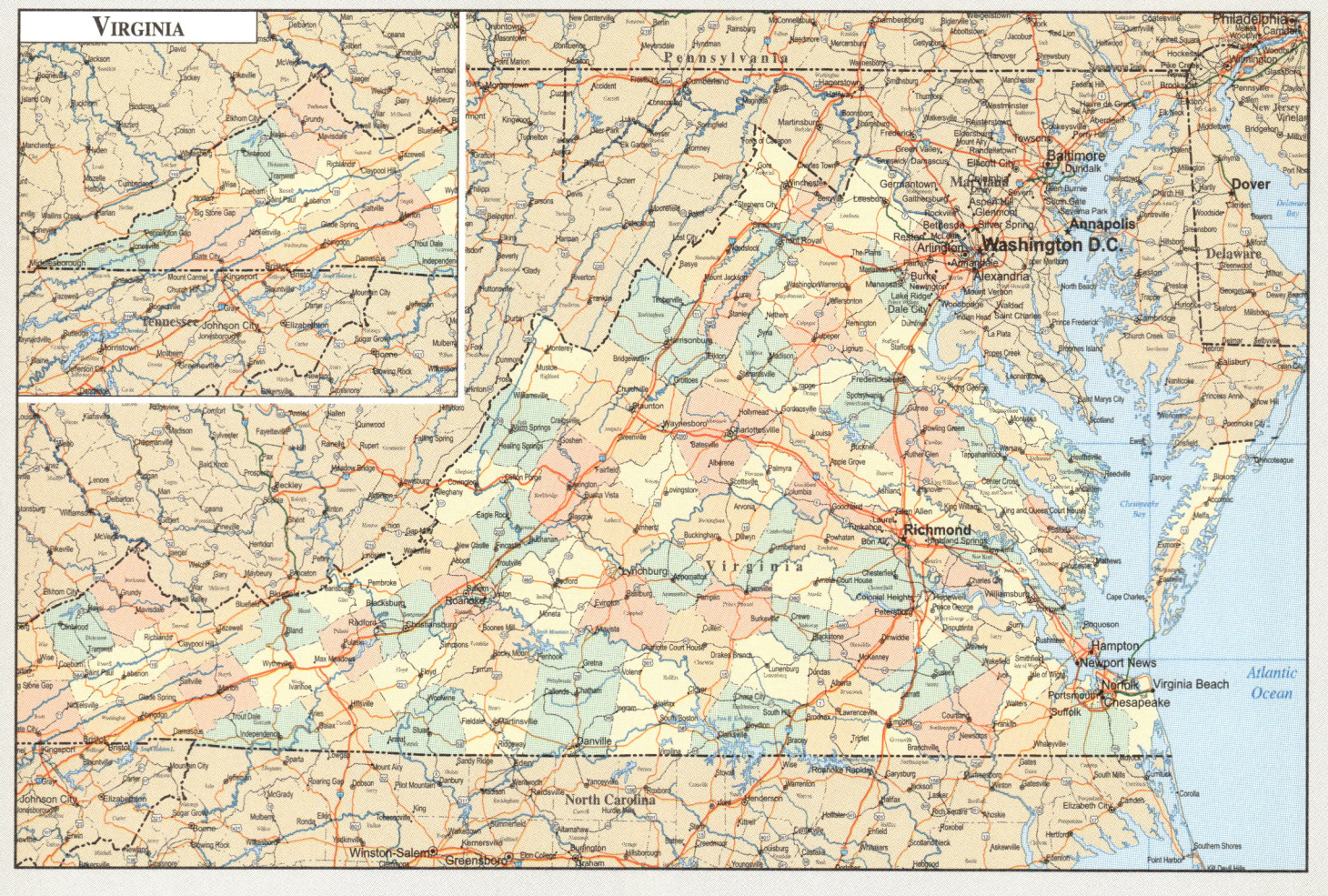

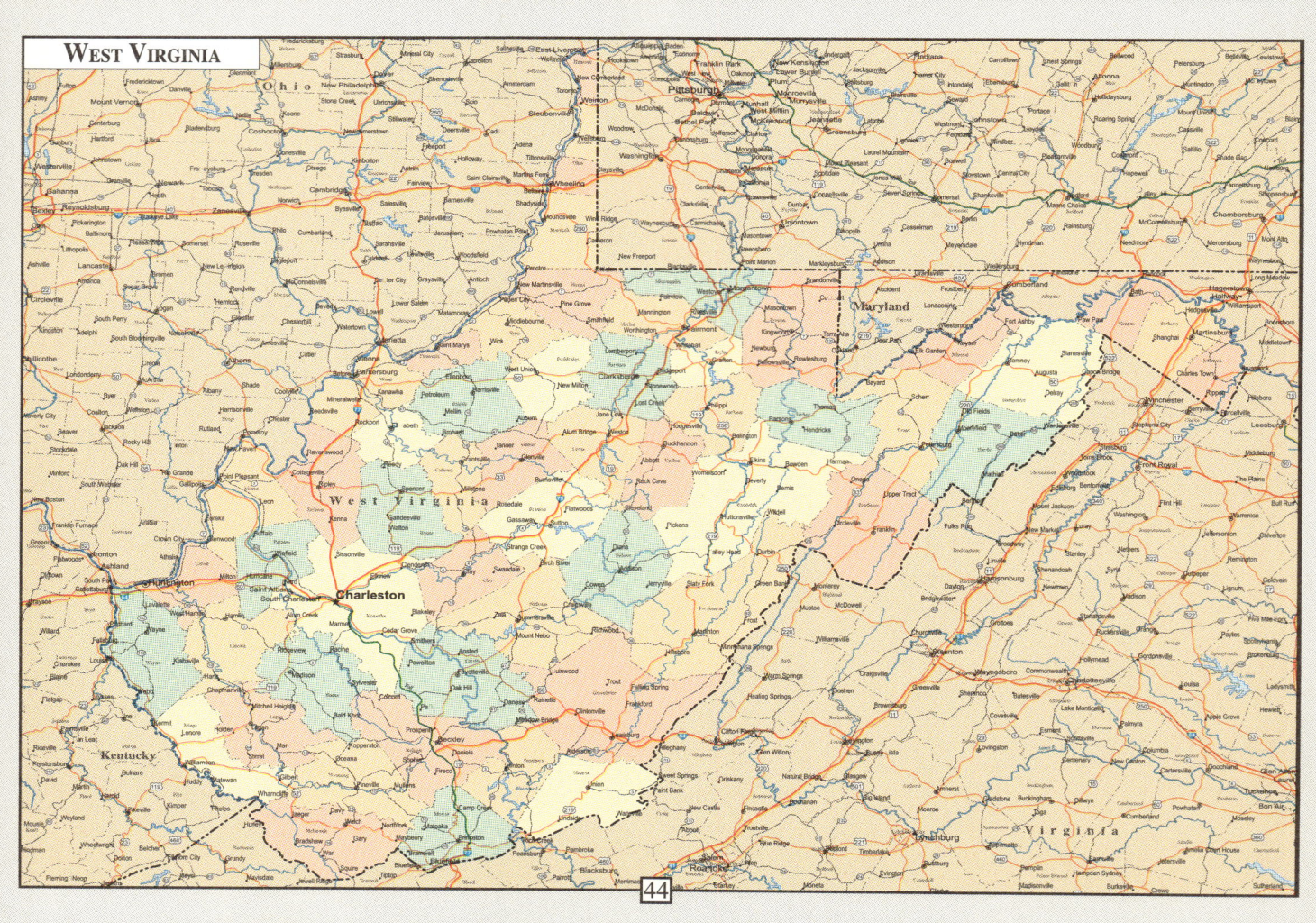

# West Virginia

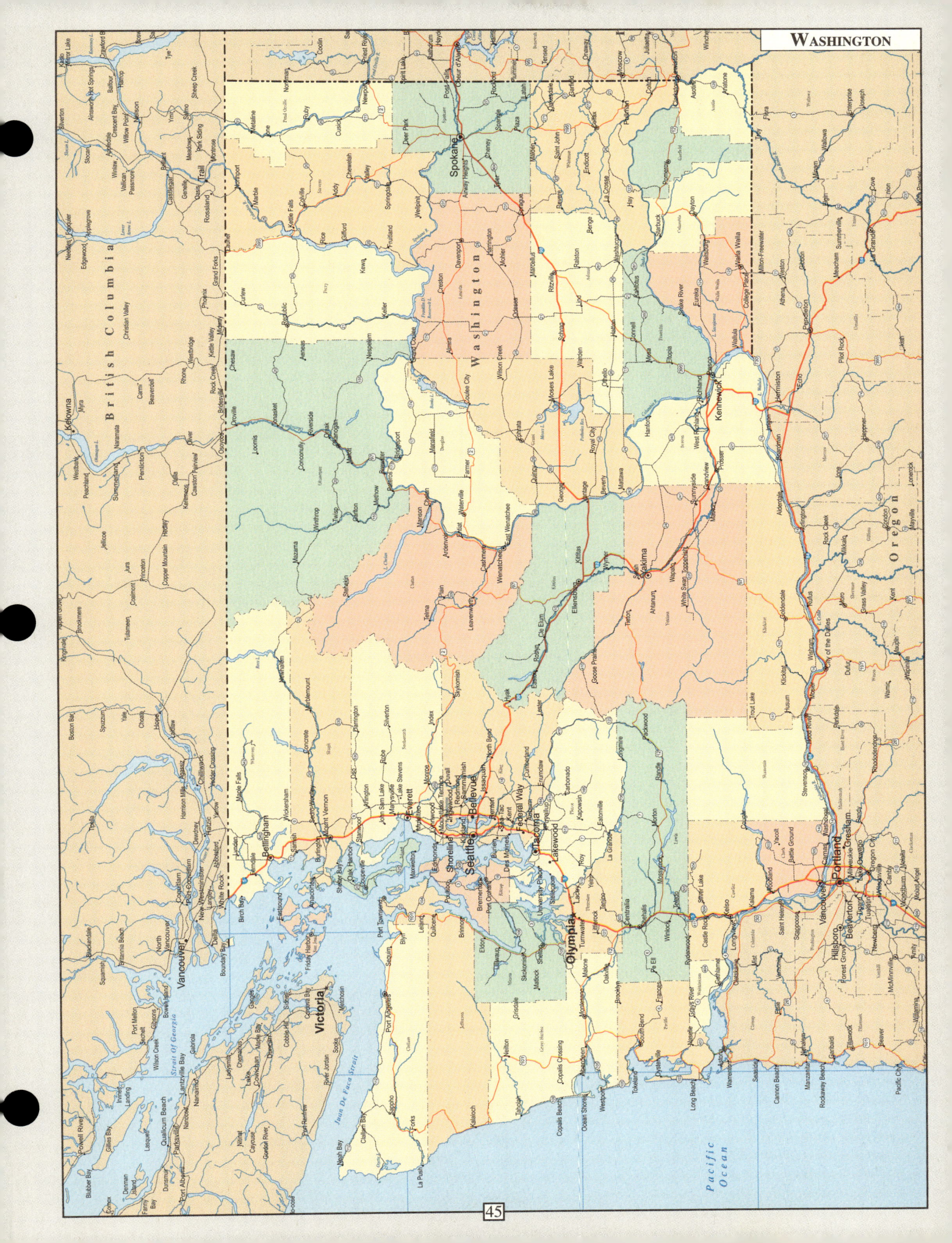

# Washington

# WISCONSIN

# Wyoming

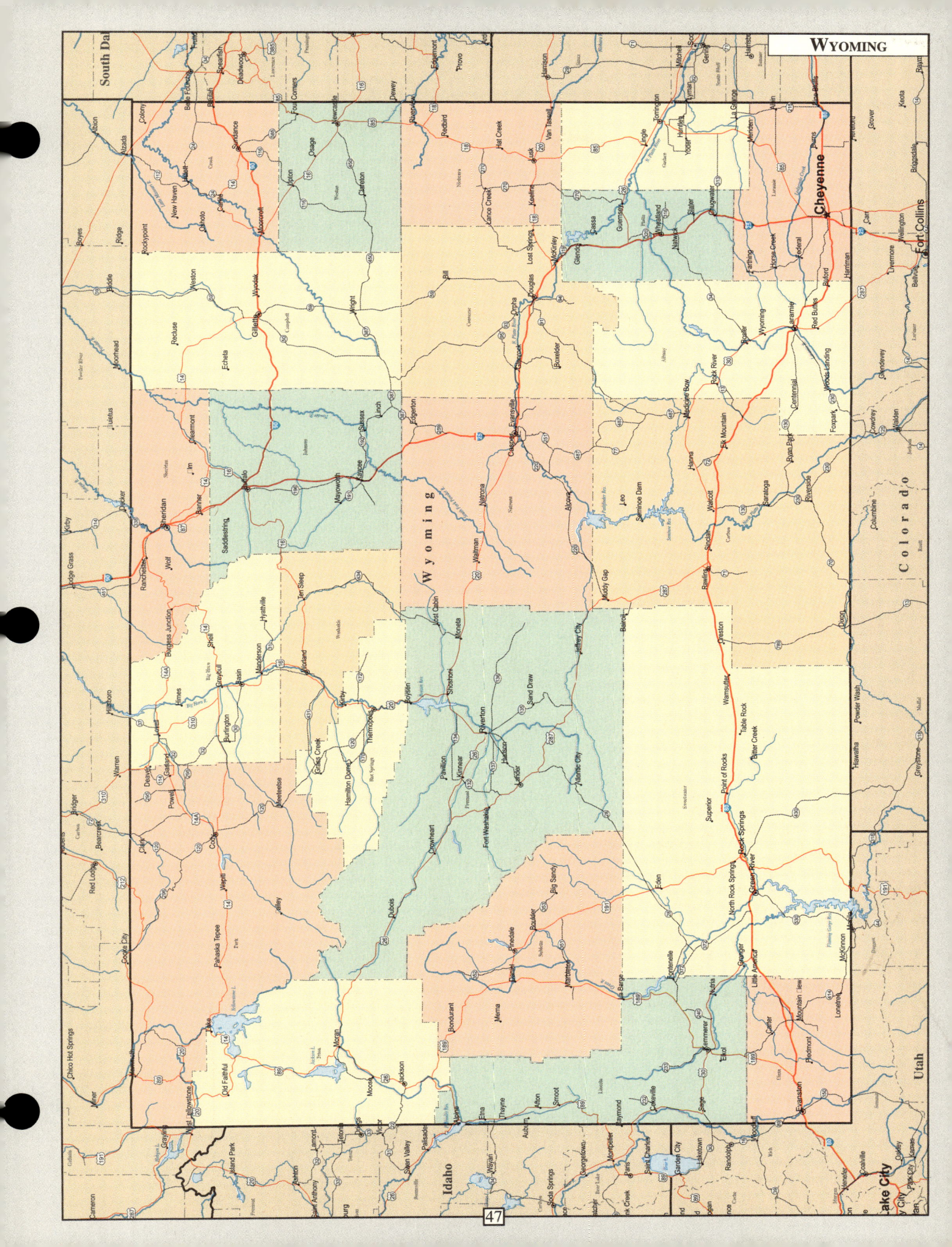

# ATLAS INDEX

| | |
|---|---|
| Alabama | 3 |
| Alaska | 4 |
| Arizona | 5 |
| Arkansas | 6 |
| California | 7 |
| Colorado | 8 |
| Connecticut | 9 |
| Delaware | 9 |
| Florida | 10 |
| Georgia | 11 |
| Hawaii | 12 |
| Idaho | 12 |
| Illinois | 13 |
| Indiana | 14 |
| Iowa | 15 |
| Kansas | 16 |
| Kentucky | 17 |
| Louisiana | 18 |
| Maine | 19 |
| Maryland | 20 |
| Massachusetts | 21 |
| Michigan | 22 |
| Minnesota | 23 |
| Mississippi | 24 |
| Missouri | 25 |
| Montana | 26 |
| Nebraska | 27 |
| Nevada | 28 |
| New Hampshire | 29 |
| New Jersey | 30 |
| New Mexico | 31 |
| New York | 32 |
| North Carolina | 33 |
| North Dakota | 34 |
| Ohio | 35 |
| Oklahoma | 36 |
| Oregon | 37 |
| Pennsylvania | 38 |
| Rhode Island | 39 |
| South Carolina | 33 |
| South Dakota | 34 |
| Tennessee | 40 |
| Texas | 41 |
| Utah | 42 |
| Vermont | 43 |
| Virginia | 44 |
| Washington | 45 |
| West Virginia | 44 |
| Wisconsin | 46 |
| Wyoming | 47 |